WEALTH WITHOUT WORRY

To Brad
with best regards,

WEALTH WITHOUT WORRY

JAMES N. WHIDDON
WITH LANCE ALSTON

BROWN BOOKS PUBLISHING GROUP

Brown Books Publishing Group
16200 N. Dallas Pkwy Ste. 170
Dallas, TX 75248

Printed in the United States of America
10 9 8 7 6 5 4 3
ISBN 1-933285-01-X
LCCN 2005925082

Attention corporations, professional organizations, and universities: quantity discounts are available on bulk purchases of this book. For information, please contact info@theinvestingrevolution.com.

Disclaimer

Dedication

To my beloved wife, Elizabeth, who chose to invest her life with mine.

And to my sons, Johnathan and Daniel,
who have brought me immeasurable wealth.

Contents

Acknowledgments

S ir Winston Churchill once said, "Writing a book is an adventure: It begins as an amusement, then it becomes a mistress, then a master, and finally a tyrant."

Truer words were never spoken.

Appreciation is first due to all the brilliant economic thinkers who have paved the way for those of us who now declare their wisdom. Work from men such as Friedrich Hayek, Harry Markowitz, William Sharpe, and Eugene Fama have forever changed our understanding of capital markets for the better. Also, many thanks to the professionals at Dimensional Fund Advisors for their vast wealth of information, their creativity and innovation and their willingness to share their wisdom with independent advisors and individual investors.

I am also grateful to investment pioneers like John Bogle and members of the media such as Jonathan Clements of the *Wall Street Journal* and syndicated columnist Scott Burns who are truly taking a stand for individual investors with their good work.

A project to compile thoughts and information in a way that can be communicated logically and effectively could never have been accomplished without the hard work and dedication of my team. Thank you, Matt Sanders, Joy Justice, Rachel Nolte, and Tyra Penn. You all deserve to have your names on the front cover. Thanks also to Cristina and Claire Alston for letting me use your husband/daddy on so many weekends. Lance, your insight, suggestions, and contributions to the book have been outstanding. I am fortunate to have such a good business partner.

Thanks to all the manuscript readers that improved this book immeasurably with their thoughtful suggestions. In particular, Gary Belsky, Daniel Solin, Larry and Janie Trantham, Tom Westerfield, Brent Smith, Scott Matthews, and John Wilks. Your interest in our efforts was both flattering and humbling. A special thanks to Alex Booras for his guidance, enthusiasm, and sound advice.

Our publisher Milli Brown and her staff at Brown Books Publishing Group helped put the polishing touches on the book and made it better than I ever believed possible. My heartfelt gratitude to you all.

I want to offer a heartfelt thank-you to our clients. Without you, there is no career, no profession, and no book. Your loyalty and relationships are what make our professional lives so fulfilling.

Thanks to the love of my life, Elizabeth, and my sons Johnathan and Daniel. You sacrificed me during the unusually long hours as I engaged in a project you knew I was passionate about. You may now have me back.

I want to say thank you to my in-laws, Dr. Jess and Packy Bescos, whom I have come to love and appreciate more each year. Thanks again for entrusting me with your precious daughter two decades ago.

Finally, thanks to Lawrence and Mary Whiddon. You raised me right and taught me many valuable lessons in both word and deed; among them this one: "That man is the wealthiest whose satisfactions are the simplest."

James N. Whiddon

Preface

A Prince whose character is thus marked by every act which may define a Tyrant, is unfit to be the ruler of a free people.

**–From the Declaration of Independence
by American statesman Thomas Jefferson**

Just as the Founding Fathers held the truths of this, America's greatest document, to be self-evident, we believe all investors should have the right to benefit from free capital markets. Over time, Wall Street autocrats have usurped Americans' rights as investors. Wall Street rulers now must be exposed for what they are—tyrants.

Capital markets were created for the benefit of those who participate in them. Whenever the leaders of capital market institutions harm those whom they exist to help, their power must be removed. When a prolonged record of abuses is evident, their methods must be exposed. When malfeasance and misleading information become overbearing, it is the right of each participant to demand fair treatment. It is time for a change.

When we ponder the historical figures who championed free capital markets, we see leaders with revolutionary ideas, which inspired drastic and far-reaching changes. We don't use "revolutionary" casually, but there is no better word to accurately convey the ideas described in this book.

The playing field must be leveled. It is time for every investor to learn how to triumph in the investing arena. There should be no losers.

Investing is not a zero-sum game. Free capital markets make it possible for everyone to win. Everyone can have a piece of the ever-expanding pie. Free markets work.

By the time you finish reading this book, you will understand the answers to the most important investing questions. As a blessed participant in the greatest economic system in the history of mankind, it is time for you to claim your inalienable prosperity. It is time for you to create wealth without worry.

I

Introduction

Where Wall Street leads, most investors blindly follow. This book is not for those followers. *Wealth Without Worry* is for investors who have always suspected that Wall Street is only interested in promoting a system that benefits Wall Street first. Any benefit to individual investors is secondary.

For the first several years of my financial services career, I was caught up in the failed Wall Street system that seeks to reach investment goals through active management. Fortunately, I was enlightened to the logic and obvious advantages of market return investing. Since then, I have made it my goal to rescue as many investors as will listen to this story.

This book was written for investors who are frustrated with the constant barrage of confusing and conflicting investment information, hit-and-miss approaches, and exaggerated return claims. It was written for those who are tired of having the worries of their financial future rob them of their life's present. For all who ever thought the odds were stacked against them in the investing game, *Wealth Without Worry* will change all that.

The ideas in these pages will not be widely accepted by the securities industry. In fact, this book will probably raise the ire of industry players as their investing methods are attacked. However, it will challenge securities professionals to scrutinize their own character and integrity and do what is right for their clients.

The first half of the book critically examines Wall Street's popular methods of portfolio management. Common investment strategies focus on improving returns through market timing and stock picking, also known as active management. Yet if these practices are so effective, why have the returns for the overwhelming majority of investors lagged well behind the market indices?

The first two chapters expose why active management is a futile exercise, efficient only to the degree that it lines the pockets of Wall Street executives and brokers. While well-aligned with Wall Street's interests, this management style is misaligned with the interests of individual investors.

The following chapter examines the natural tendency of most investors to chase returns. This is, of course, a direct result of subscribing to the idea that they can successfully time and pick the market. But investors consistently arrive at the party late. The performance they seek has already occurred. Chasing higher returns causes investors to buy high and sell low, and it typically results in netting less than half the market index returns.

The second half of the book offers the solution, which begins with selecting the appropriate investment help. It is important for investors to understand what type of advisor to use and what services that advisor should offer. Our "Seven Essential Questions to Ask When Interviewing an Advisor" spells out some important selection guidelines.

Chapter 5 proves that market returns are there for the taking. The discussion will encourage readers to place their faith in the economic miracle of capitalism rather than in human soothsaying. All investors can have a long-term successful investing experience by not succumbing to the Wall Street shell games.

Then come the finishing touches on achieving proper portfolio management for the ages. An overview of proper portfolio arrangement will focus on constructing the Market Return Portfolio, diversifying and allocating assets, and evaluating investment vehicles—including the one alternative we belicve is best.

Lastly, the conclusion in chapter 7 provides three action items to pursue immediately. It also provides logical answers to questions like "Why haven't I heard this before?" and "Why isn't everyone doing this?" and exposes the dubious system that the Wall Street tyrants now conceal.

This book explains how market returns can be harnessed simply and consistently. It provides a road map to investing success and shows how the solution does not lie in some new scheme, but rather that the answers have always been there. *Wealth Without Worry* will give you the tools to finally obtain financial independence and peace of mind—a gift that is priceless.

Part I:
Wall Street's Failed Methods

*But such is the irresistible nature of truth, that all
it asks, and all it wants, is the liberty of appearing.*

—Thomas Paine

1 Chapter
Market Timing

Mr. and Mrs. Jones are a very intelligent, well-educated couple who like to think they are pretty good at making important decisions, including those that have a lasting effect on their retirement nest egg. For example, they made an investment decision to get back into the stock market in late 1994, after patiently waiting for the market cycle to reach the bottom. In March 2000, the Joneses decided that the bull had run its course and it was time to get out of the market completely. They did so, to their great advantage, as the markets went into a thirty-one-month dive. In November 2002, the Joneses decided correctly again and invested all of their money back into the market as a new run-up in stock prices began. Today, they continue to know just when to get into and out of the market by making intelligent decisions based on obvious market data.

Clearly this is a fantasy.

People can't predict the future. We all know this on an intellectual level. So why do so many believe the investment world is different? Because investors want to believe it.

If market timing were possible, the investment accounts of Americans would not have fallen by trillions of dollars from March 2000 to November 2002; the worst bear market since the Great Depression.

We learn at an early age that hindsight is 20/20, yet there is a lingering belief that we may be different somehow—a belief that perhaps our makeup allows us to analyze and predict accurately when it comes to securities markets. This behavioral characteristic in the financial world is known as hindsight bias: the concept that we can predict future events

3

rationally based on the information we have concerning past events. Yet a disclaimer, such as "past performance is no guarantee of future results," is required by law on investment literature and prospectuses. We all know that, absent dumb luck, we must have foreknowledge in order to profit from a race that has yet to be run.

Market timing is a cornerstone of an ineffective philosophy known as active portfolio management. The word active is often misconstrued as having a positive connotation. After all, investors expect their brokers to do something. They certainly do not want them to sit around and do nothing. Being active implies that brokers are indeed making positive things happen in the portfolios that are under their supervision. However, the more active a broker is with an account, the less likely positive things will occur.

The idea that markets can be timed successfully is perhaps the easiest investing untruth to lay bare. Many investors and brokers say they know when to enter or leave the market. At some point they must come to the realization that they do not and cannot know where the markets are going.

NOTED EXPERTS ON MARKET TIMING

Investment legend Peter Lynch was once quoted as saying, "Attempting to forecast whether the market is at a peak or in a valley— and whether to buy or unload stocks as a result—is a waste of time. I don't know anyone who has been right more than once in a row."[1]

This man is regarded by many as one of the great investment gurus of our time. If ever there was a great stock market timer, it was Peter Lynch. Yet Lynch clearly implies that the timing game cannot be won. And as you look a little deeper into his statement you see the wisdom of it. In order to time the market successfully, one must indeed be right at least twice in a row. You must know when to get in and when to get out or when to get out and when to get back in. If you miss on either decision, you lose.

Another famous investment industry pioneer, Vanguard Group founder John Bogle, said, "In thirty years in the business, I do not know anyone who knows anyone who has [timed the market] successfully and consistently.

My impression is that trying to do market timing is likely not only not to add value to your investment program, but also to be counterproductive."[2]

THE MEDIA'S ROLE

Market timing is also a media darling. Nearly every major financial publication and broadcast in the country is based, at least in part, upon the premise that successfully timing the market is a possibility. "Why You Should Own Technology Stocks Now" and "The Coming Market Boom (or Bust)" are examples of common headlines that attract investors like moths to a porch light on a warm summer evening. They promote the belief that timing the market is within the average investor's grasp.

It is not hard to understand why investors make poor decisions when they rely on the daily news for their investment advice. In all fairness, I do not believe that the financial media are trying to mislead anyone. Most members of the media are well-intentioned, honest citizens. Their job is to report the news or opinions of the day, not to give financial advice. These are two very different propositions.

The trouble is that many investors misconstrue the news of the day (or random opinions) as advice. This speaks to the tremendous influence the mass media have in our lives. So while the daily news can be interesting and fun to talk about around the water cooler or at the kitchen table, it rarely has a lasting effect on capital markets.

THE MARKET HATES UNCERTAINTY

There is nothing more fickle than the securities markets. An example of this fickleness and unpredictability came with the days leading up to the 2003 start of the war with Iraq.

On March 13, news came out that the war with Iraq could be delayed or perhaps even avoided. There were rumors of Iraqi generals wanting to surrender before the first shot was fired. The Dow Jones industrial average exploded by 269.68 points that day. Four days later, on March 17,

---

war was imminent, and the Dow shot up again with an increase of 282.2 points. This example illustrates how the market doesn't hate war or other calamitous events as much as it hates uncertainty. The market looked upon these two opposite developments as positive for stocks because closure on the important war issue potentially was at hand. Go figure.

WIDELY USED TIMING TECHNIQUES

One common tool used to time market sectors and individual securities is technical analysis, which involves making and interpreting stock charts. (Those who engage in this activity are sometimes called chartists.) Technical analysis is something we see quite often in newsletters dedicated to timing. These publications claim that charting offers a scientific way to make logical market decisions.

In a discussion of technical analysis we might talk about a bullish trend, or an upward movement in stock price, charted as in Figure 1.1. A bearish trend heads in the opposite direction.

Figure 1.1

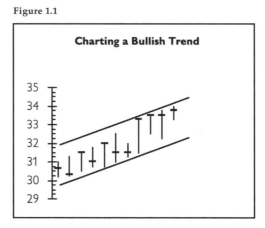

Or perhaps we would hear about the shoulders formed from the market's slight up-and-down movements that eventually form a neckline. Breaking the neckline is said to be a bearish signal (see Figure 1.2).

Figure 1.2

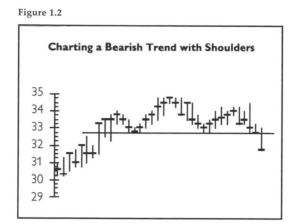

Charting is simply a matter of connecting the dots to find distinguishable patterns of prices on which to make predictions. All of this is designed to bring about a feeling that some detailed work and analysis have taken place.

Such a tracking technique clearly appeals to an investor who is more interested in profits from daily trading versus long-term investing. But this is a failed strategy for two reasons:

1. **No secrets.** If charting worked as well as some advisors argue, then the playground would get very crowded. The buy or sell indicator would be of little value if many others were acting on the same information.

2. **Randomness.** The chartist relies on his or her ability to read changes in direction or status of a stock price or market. As we'll discuss, the price of a stock is dependent on many random factors that usually occur somewhat rapidly—sometimes *very* rapidly.

Even if charts are coded rigorously into a computer and then tested, they produce no statistical basis for making money; they are simply a tangible illustration of wishful thinking. Chartists' reliance on the momentum to change before making a trading decision will more times than not leave them standing at the station as the train leaves.

DATA MINING

Data mining is another common technique among market timers. Sometimes called data snooping, it is a methodology that can look very much like a credible way of arriving at investment decisions. For example, data miners might consider prevailing interest rates or industrial production in relation to stock market performance over an extended period of time. With many charts and graphs at their side, data miners may proceed to make a compelling case for an important investment move or strategy. However, at their core, data miners still are involved with market timing and have little or no reliable evidence to support a claim that their methods work consistently over the long term.

When it comes to data mining, almost anything can be used to prove a point. If you are a sports fan, you may recall an instance of data mining that was well-publicized a few years ago when it was discovered that each time the NFC team defeated the AFC team in the Super Bowl, we could expect an up year in the stock market. Where did this crazy notion come from? Well, for several years the pattern held true, and thus someone noted it. Others have referenced hemlines, sunspots, and even butter production in Bangladesh as reliable indicators of market direction.

When it comes to data mining, the famous quote from Mark Twain holds true:

> *Figures often beguile me, particularly when I have the arranging of them myself; in which case the remark attributed to Disraeli would often apply with justice and force: "There are three kinds of lies: lies, damned lies, and statistics."*[3]

> —**From *Autobiography of Mark Twain***

TIMING NEWSLETTERS

Newsletters and other publications dedicated to market timing are popular among the investing public as individuals try to decide their next investing moves. Evidence suggests that these publications are some of the worst of all possible sources for investment advice. There are hundreds of these timing publications in the United States, ranging from the barely plausible to the absurd, with an average monthly subscription cost of $100 to $300. The fact that most are published monthly begs the question: With news changing by the minute, how timely can monthly advice be?

Timing newsletters are notorious for charting (technical analysis) and data mining. Unfortunately, some of these publications occasionally offer winning advice. We say "unfortunately" because this occasional correct guess leads the public to believe that the writers are skilled in the art of timing the market. But market timing newsletters, not ironically, get it right about as often as "professional" money managers.

Noted author, analyst, and money manager David Dreman tracked the opinions of market prognosticators dating back to 1929. He found them to be correct only about 23 percent of the time.[4] A coin-flipper will be right 50 percent of the time! Yet the publications continue to thrive as investors think they are different somehow.

When a newsletter hits it right, even one time, its authors tend to live on the success for years—even decades. The trouble is that readers suffer because they put their faith in the publication's information, based on one pick or a short run of successes. (Remember Peter Lynch's quote on being right more than once in a row?) Yet what do these proxy advisors really have on the line other than the loss of another subscriber? With so many investors having the lottery mentality of hitting it big and ultrashort memories, these timing newsletter publishers will always have plenty of revenue.

MUTUAL FUND MARKET TIMERS

A 2004 study by Dalbar Inc., a leading financial-services market research firm, indicates just how devastating timing strategies in the mutual fund arena can be. Dalbar examined the flows into and out of mutual funds for the previous twenty years and found that market timers in stock funds lost an average of 3.29 percent per year. During this same period, the Standard & Poor's 500 Index (S&P 500)[5] grew by 12.98 percent annually. The average investor (timers and nontimers) earned 3.51 percent per year.

Dalbar President Lou Harvey commented, "This finding is consistent with the well-known behavior of investors to brag about their gains but remain silent about losses. The occasional money makers create the illusion that all timers are winners all the time. The fact is that most timers lose money most often, and this data now confirms it."

NO TIMING ADVANTAGE

Figure 1.3 shows three very different investment timing results. Each of the three is supposed to have invested systematically in the S&P 500 once per quarter for thirty years ending in 2004.[6]

Loser Lenny tried to time his deposits just right. Unfortunately, he bought on the worst possible day (highest price) each quarter during the thirty-year period. He had perfectly bad timing. Fortunate Fran bought the same amount on the best possible day (lowest price) for the same time period. She had perfectly good timing for 120 straight quarters. Steady Eddie did not use any timing technique and simply set up an automatic investment program without any regard whatsoever to the market conditions. In other words, he put the money in on the first day of the quarter and said, "I'll check it in thirty years." The results are striking.

Figure 1.3

S&P 500: Quarterly Investing Best and Worst Days, 1975 to 2004	
Loser Lenny (buys at high)	9.1 percent
Fortunate Fran (buys at low)	9.6 percent
Steady Eddie (first day of quarter)	9.4 percent

The fact that over a thirty-year period, the difference between a perfectly bad timer and a perfectly good timer is only about half a percent is phenomenal. We can only reason that since there are no perfect timers in either direction—good or bad—any timing attempts will average out over the long run. That is exactly what happened here.

TIME IN THE MARKET IS EVERYTHING!

Market timing still enjoys great appeal. Yet the case against this investing technique grows stronger each day. Recent data show the utter futility of trying to guess what will happen in the securities markets.[7]

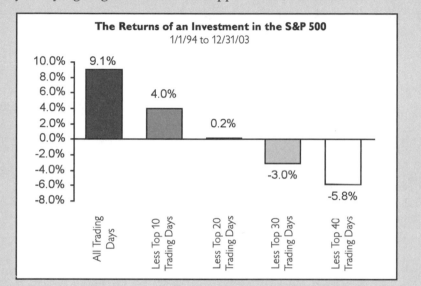

The Returns of an Investment in the S&P 500
1/1/94 to 12/31/03

This graph shows how missing only a few of the market's best days would have a huge negative effect on the returns of an investment in the S&P 500 Index during this ten-year period. The most dramatic message from the chart is that if you had missed the best forty days (a little more than 1 percent) out of the more than 3,600 days of that period, you would have lost 5.8 percent per year versus gaining 9.1 percent per year if you had stayed in for the entire time. That is a 14.9 percent difference! (Please keep in mind this time period represents some of the best and worst years in market history.) So given this evidence, why would any prudent investor sit on the sidelines and wave at those still marching in the market parade? The answer is panic, pure and simple. Investors see the storm clouds around them (pending war, economic slump, etc.) and take their eyes off the goal. History tells us that staying the course is the only sensible way to proceed. The talking head investment analysts all say something different depending on what bubble they think will burst next. The media unwittingly contribute to the volatile atmosphere by reporting mostly bad news because good news does not sell copies. What do investors think other than the sky is falling? Investors run for cover in cash and fixed-income instruments and out of equities because they see bonds as a traditionally safe investment vehicle. This presumably will calm their nerves and enable them to avoid the declining stock market. This safety will be only an illusion, not a reality. Unfortunately, this fact will be learned too late for most.

So what to do? The alternative to market timing is long-term, steadfast investing. Adhering to an investment policy statement (IPS) regardless of short-term fluctuations eliminates any guesswork. An IPS is a written document that defines your objectives and constraints and helps maintain a sound long-term plan, even when short-term market movements cause second-guessing. Once your IPS is complete, it will:

- Define the appropriate level of risk for your situation
- Establish the expected investment time horizon
- Determine the rate of return needed based on retirement cash flow needs
- Prescribe the asset classes to be used
- Document the investment methodology used in managing your portfolio
- Help determine the means for making any adjustments to your current portfolio

Giving way to fear will undermine your investment program. There may be times and circumstances when you need an adjustment in your asset allocation, but make sure this decision stems from the long-term strategy as outlined in your plan and not from overconfidence in your ability to predict market movements. Whenever you become tense about markets, review the historical data to regain your confidence in your long-term strategy, and remember this simple thought: It is not timing the market, but time in the market that brings long-term investment success.

The message: Don't watch markets or try to time them—just be *in* them.

DEALING WITH MACRO ECONOMIC FORECASTS

On December 5, 1996, Federal Reserve Chairman Alan Greenspan made his famous "irrational exuberance" speech, in which he warned of an overheating market, based on inflated valuations, and the possibility of an "unexpected and prolonged contraction" à la Japan.[8] The S&P 500 Index proceeded to grow for the next three and a quarter years from 744 to a peak of 1,527 on March 23, 2000.

Greenspan was right about the bubble bursting—the only trouble is that it was more than three years later. The index then dropped steadily, hitting a low of 776 on October 9, 2002, before it once again changed directions. This two-and-a-half-year period of market decline was hardly the Japanotype contraction of which Greenspan warned.

So why did Greenspan have such poor timing on his prognostication? Is there anyone on Earth who has better financial data and resources at his disposal to make forecasts? If Greenspan does not have the ability, should we believe that there are money managers who can predict market movements accurately so as to benefit their clients? And if they did, would they be inclined to share this kind of information?

A PERFECT MARKET FOR TIMERS?

Many market-timing brokers and newsletter writers proclaim that their real value is most apparent in turbulent, fast-moving markets. In the last decade, we have had a perfect laboratory in which to test the real value of professional money managers. Figure 1.4 shows a three-plus-year bull market and a two-and-a-half-year decline, followed by another fourteen-month run-up.

Figure 1.4

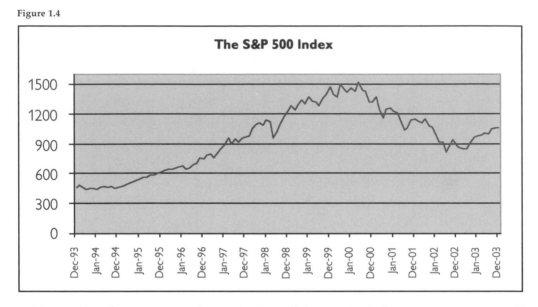

How did the experts fare during this period that was supposedly perfect for timers?

- The S&P 500 Index average annualized return was 10.97 percent.[9]

- The average annualized return for active US large cap fund managers was 9.19 percent.[10]

- The percentage of US large cap active managers that beat the S&P 500 Index was less than one out of four (23.7 percent).[11]

Clearly there is a limit to any success that can be gleaned from market-timing strategies. A market timer's best efforts usually are no match for the randomness of the market.

ESCAPING A BEAR MARKET

In the midst of any bear market, there is a nagging temptation to either sneak out of the markets or engage in an all-out mad dash to the hills, seeking refuge from the storm in the form of bonds or cash equivalents. The question on everyone's mind is: "When will it all end?" Ironically, more often than not, the darker the mood of the masses, the nearer the end we are.

There's certainly no stronger evidence of that mood than in the media's coverage of bear markets. We should be reminded that the news in the investing world is rarely, if ever, all bad—even in the worst of times, like those we experienced from March 2000 through October 2002. Investors who implement maximum diversification and ignore timing techniques can actually gain ground in some asset classes during a market downturn. (Small US value, for example, gained 16.11 percent as represented by the Russell 2000 Value Index during the March 2000 to October 2002 time period.) While this may not completely spare investor portfolios from the claw of a bear market, it will most certainly result in a buffering effect allowing most, if not all, long-term financial objectives to remain intact.

In spite of dark economic clouds that appear occasionally, the best time to buy equities is always now. As long as the world turns; families grow; children need food, clothing, shelter, and education; and the entrepreneurial spirit thrives, an economy—and thus the markets—must grow.

Owning stocks is the best way to effectively hedge against inflation—and its evil twin, taxation—and create long-term wealth. We know the long-term, after-inflation, after-tax historical return of stocks over bonds is approximately three to one. Regardless of any climate in the financial markets, those numbers defy argument.

While seeking refuge in bonds or cash may provide some restful nights in the short term, it is (due to opportunity costs) an extremely expensive sleep aid.

The only sure way to miss out on the tremendous gains that follow a market downturn is to exit the game before it is over. Stay focused on your goals, keep that investment chin up, and stay in the market!

WHY MARKET TIMING DOESN'T WORK

We've shown several examples and discussed the failings of market timing as a long-term strategy. The fundamental reason it is impossible to consistently time the market is that the securities markets are efficient. Consider the following:

1. **Rapid communication.** The age in which we live affords instantaneous access to accurate data. This fact supports the idea of how difficult it is to get an edge on anyone concerning the receipt of information. Perhaps before the computer age came about, we could learn something about an investment idea that would provide a small window of opportunity for profit. But with the advent of the personal computer, that opportunity has all but vanished even for the professional.

2. **Financial analysts act immediately.** Because the information is so readily available, intelligent, eager analysts are well-equipped to act. The problem with this is that any data, no matter how accurate, cannot be acted upon in a timely fashion so as to gain an advantage. Ironically, these analysts are all so good at what they do that they cancel out one another's efforts. We call this the efficient analyst paradox. The more numerous the competitors, the less likely one will achieve superior results.

3. **New information.** The news is inherently unpredictable. One needs only to look at any financial news channel on a weekday to see this exhibited. On the television screen (usually at the bottom), there is a ticker that changes every three seconds to reflect that this new information has been processed into the market. As a result, the price of any one stock or market reflects all the known information at that moment in time. So to select undervalued stocks at the right time consistently is extremely difficult.

4. **Random events.** Events that have nothing to do with the intrinsic financial health of companies can dramatically influence their stock prices. We need to go no further than September 11, 2001, to understand this truth in its purest form. While the airline industry was on shaky financial footing before this horrific event, could it ever have dreamed of, much less controlled, the negative effect the tragedies would have on the financial world? Conversely, companies in the homeland security industry have seen a boon from the unfortunate results of this attack. Other events like oil embargoes, natural disasters, and tax legislation also can influence stock prices—allowing absolutely no control to analysts or investors.

SUMMARY

In a dynamic capitalist economy, market timing is a fool's errand. By looking closer at market timing techniques through a common-sense lens, we can see that they are simply decoys designed to distract us from reality. We have shown how the data expose randomness in market fluctuations that cannot be controlled or predicted by mere humans. Furthermore, when faced with the facts surrounding the efficiency of the securities markets and the uncertainty of arbitrary events, logic dictates that timing the market is ineffective. In short, time in the market, regardless of market conditions or undulations, will ultimately provide the return and purchasing power protection that an investor needs to succeed.

Chapter 2

Stock Picking

The second failed component of active portfolio management is stock picking. While many brokers and investment managers would admit that timing the market is a fool's struggle, almost all of them subscribe to the theory that winning stocks can be picked successfully. The fallacy of this assumption is that this means someone else—most everyone else (i.e., the market)—must be wrong. We must ask ourselves: What are the chances of that being the case? This entire picking concept is nothing more than speculation; it is not investing.

Speculation involves the idea that you cast your lot with a particular security or sector (such as technology), and then you either win or you lose. There is no middle ground. There is nothing wrong with speculation as long as you understand the risks, but do not confuse speculating with investing.

Investing involves understanding the concept that everyone can be a winner. Yes, that means everyone can have a piece of an ever-expanding pie. Every investor can have a successful experience. With capitalism, market returns are essentially there for the taking. Investing is not a zero-sum game.

We will have more to say about investing in later chapters. Let's now look closer at the concept of stock picking, and why, like market timing, security selection techniques are largely an exercise in futility.

FUNDAMENTAL STOCK ANALYSIS

Fundamental analysis is a favorite of stock pickers. In fact, the overwhelming majority of security analysts consider themselves fundamental analysts. You may recall that technical analysis involves using historical data to devise market timing strategies. Fundamental analysis takes a different approach.

Fundamental analysts care little about the past price pattern of a stock or market and would rather focus on determining a company's proper inherent or fundamental value. This involves trying to ascertain what a stock is really worth. The idea here is to make some definitive distinction between a stock's current price and its true value. Analysts will pore over past financial numbers trying to estimate future earnings and dividends; they will take a close look at all the various financial ratios and conduct personal interviews with management during site visits. These activities will supposedly give analysts the tools they need to do the job well and determine if a buy, sell, or hold recommendation is warranted.

However, in a study conducted for the National Bureau of Economic Research (NBER), the authors found that market analysts correctly predicted price targets slightly more than 50 percent of the time (coin flip). Furthermore, when the analysts missed their targets, they did so by more than 15 percent on average and in some cases much more.[1]

The basic problem with the fundamental analysis approach is the fact that various factors are uncontrollable. Consider these reasons why this is so.

- **Financial data are historical in nature.** Old numbers have questionable value for predicting the future. Continual revisions make the task even more daunting.

- **Market risk comes into play.** What affects the market as a whole may override any predicted pricing based on the value assessment of one company.

- **Analysts are human.** They may just miss on their assessment in spite of accurate data.

- **The CEO factor is real.** Even with perfect analysis, the actions of an unscrupulous or careless executive may sink the entire company.

- **Consistency is important.** If the methodology is successful once, can analysts be successful again and again—to the extent that they must be in order to populate a properly diversified portfolio? The data overwhelmingly suggest they cannot.

To clarify this last point, let's take a look at typical active mutual fund managers. They almost certainly will use fundamental analysis to assess the potential buys and sells in their funds. If professional stock pickers are going to tout their skills of selection as their unique ability, they should naturally be willing to stand by their picks down to a relatively short list of positions. As they look at a group of stocks, the S&P 500 for example, they presumably would have the ability to sift this number down to the one hundred best through careful analysis and perhaps a proprietary selection methodology. But why stop there? Could they not then use the same analysis to pare the group down to the best fifty? What about the best twenty-five of that group? Or even all the way down to the best ten companies in the S&P 500. Would an investor be willing to put all of his or her money in these ten stocks? We would hope not. It is unlikely that the fund manager would, either.

We know this "ten-best-stocks" proclamation is rarely made by actual money managers because they prefer to have a larger number of stocks to hedge their own bets against picking mistakes. (The word "bet" is used purposely here.) They do not believe in their systems of selection enough to go out on a limb with just ten stocks—or even twenty-five stocks in most cases. Therefore, they are likely to place many other stocks in their portfolios for insulation. This is one reason why we see many funds that have identical positions in their portfolios—particularly within the same fund family. We call this fund overlap. This duplication of positions within a portfolio is in direct opposition to the concept of proper diversification. Yet these money managers will continue to boast of their superior picking acumen.

Unfortunately, when headlines in financial publications announce "The Ten Best Stocks for This Year," many investors take it seriously. Simple math tells us that picking the best ten out of the thousands of stocks on the exchanges today is an even lower probability than the ten best stocks in the S&P 500 scenario we just discussed. In reality, these writers have no idea what the future holds for their top ten. We hope that no reasonable investor will act on such advice and will realize that articles of this nature have more entertainment value than anything else.

THE CEO FACTOR

Let's say for a moment that your professional money manager buys and sells individual securities in your account on a regular basis. An in-depth analysis on a particular stock has been done. Your money manager understands the company's business model, knows its products, and has talked to its suppliers and the management team. In fact, your money manager has even conducted technical research on the price movement of the stock. It looks like a great stock and you are ready to buy, but you've forgotten one unknowable that could ruin your investment: the CEO factor.

The CEO factor has become a critical variable in the stock picking game. Some people may contend that this factor has always been present. But certainly with the advent of problems reported in the media, such as those with Enron and WorldCom, it is now undoubtedly a factor to be considered. Whether the problem is phantom revenue, mislabeled expenses, hidden loans or fictitious companies, these games can make all of the research useless and cause the stock price to plummet overnight. No amount of information can help an outside speculator if the leaders on the inside aren't playing the game fairly. So how do investors deal with this factor?

There are two primary risks in owning a stock. One is the systematic risk inherent in the stock market as a whole—called market risk. We cannot avoid this risk if we choose to own equities—and equities are the only way for the individual investor to create long-term wealth. Hence, investors must accept market risk.

> The second investment risk is classified as nonsystematic or individual stock risk, which is where the CEO factor looms so large. The solution to this risk is diversification—holding a multitude of stocks within each asset class in your portfolio. This does not change the risk in any specific stock you own; however, it does minimize the influence on your whole portfolio if one stock plummets. But how many stocks do you need to be sufficiently diversified?
>
> How about all of them?

NOT ENOUGH GURUS

Warren Buffet and Peter Lynch are perhaps two of the most notable figures who come to mind when we think of stock-picking gurus. They both have received accolades for their prowess and have earned many investors nice returns during their tenures. Let's take a look at their results:

- Warren Buffet's often entertaining and sometimes controversial annual report is a must-read in financial circles. His operating company, Berkshire Hathaway, had a combined annualized return of 22.2 percent from 1965 through 2003 compared with 10.5 percent for the S&P 500 Index. This difference is impressive by any measure. However, when we look at the volatility of the company, we see time periods such as from late 1999 to the spring of 2000 where it lost almost half of its value while the broad markets were experiencing double-digit returns. Hardly a place for the risk-averse investor. It is interesting that, in his 2003 annual report, Buffet wrote, "Overall, we are certain Berkshire's performance in the future will fall far short of what it has been in the past."[2] Berkshire Hathaway class B stock returned 4.3 percent for the calendar year 2004.

- Lynch's success was more short-lived in the nine years ending in early 1990. With the tremendous marketing muscle of Fidelity behind him, Lynch grew the Magellan Fund to the world's largest mutual fund. His annualized return for Magellan was 22.5 percent[3] compared with 16.5 percent for the S&P 500 Index. While this is an excellent track record, recent data show that about one in four of the surviving large cap US mutual funds also beat the S&P 500 return for the last ten years ending in 2004. On average they beat it by 1.64 percent per year. The other 75.9 percent of funds underperformed by an average of 2.66 percent per year. However, only four funds out of 482 with ten-year track records outperformed the S&P 500 by Lynch's margin.[4] We might say this represents a 0.8 percent chance of finding another Peter Lynch before the fact.

As we consider these two phenomenal managers, it should be pointed out that they are only two. Only two that have become household names among the general public. Two out of thousands and thousands of money managers who have come and gone. Two who are not likely to take your phone call.

Furthermore, the chances of anyone selecting enough gurus to cover each of six to fifteen asset classes (as proper diversification demands) are minuscule. So while we may have witnessed some greatness in these two fellows—how many Tiger Woodses of money management are there in the world? In our lifetime?

PICKS IN THE POPULAR MEDIA

To illustrate the ineffectiveness of the stock picking game, we turn to the print media. In the August 14, 2000, issue of *Fortune* magazine, billed as the "Special Investors Issue: Retire Rich," there was an article titled "Ten Stocks to Last a Decade," by David Rynecki.[5] This quote was contained therein:

> Fortune *first identified four sweeping trends that we think have the potential to transform the economy. . . . So for help in finding the stocks best positioned to capitalize on these four trends, we sought out some of the top stock pickers in the country. . . . We also did our own due diligence by poring through financial statements, talking to companies, and giving their products a test run. The result: ten stocks that*

we think will be winners over the coming decade. We've included some household names but also a few surprises. They all share exceptional management and an ability to execute no matter what happens in the macro-economy—characteristics we think will be even more important if the economy slows and investors put a premium on those companies that post consistent numbers.

This information gives a credible and serious impression. Phrases such as "sweeping trends," "top stock pickers," and "due diligence" sound very important and official. Figure 2.1 shows the ten stocks chosen, along with the S&P 500 Index, and their price changes from August 1, 2000, through December 31, 2004.[6]

Figure 2.1

Stock	% Change
Genentech	43.15%
S&P 500	-9.03%
Morgan Stanley DW	-35.79%
Viacom Class B	-44.80%
Univision	-52.89%
Nokia	-63.37%
Oracle	-63.50%
Charles Schwab	-66.43%
Broadcom	-85.61%
Nortel	-95.31%
Enron	-99.99%

All but one of the recommendations lagged behind the S&P 500 Index by a significant margin. The group had an abysmal combined annualized return of -17.12 percent for the period. A $100,000 portfolio divided equally among each of the 10 stocks would have shrunk to $43,814 during this 53-month time frame. Enron in particular is not likely to offer much help to the group anytime soon.

SPLITTING THE DECK

Consider the following scenario:

A stock broker places cold calls to one hundred people. He asks fifty of them to invest a nominal amount in a certain stock—say ABC Company. This recommendation, he states, is based on carefully analyzed data of the firm and the industry sector using the very best fundamental analysis techniques. He reiterates several times the unique qualifications his analysts have in this particular niche. The story is compelling. (Never mind the unusual rapidity with which he tells this story.) The fifty unwary investors follow his recommendation.

The same broker then calls another fifty investors and recommends a different company—say XYZ Company. He tells a similar story and the investors follow the advice—again he asks for only a nominal investment at this time.

Perhaps a month later, when a winner between the two stocks has emerged, the broker then calls half of the fifty investors who hold the better performing of the two previous stocks and makes another recommendation with the same type of story. To the other half he makes a different recommendation and follows the same procedure. The fifty investors who hold the loser of the two original recommended stocks are ignored forever.

This splitting the deck technique is followed until at last the broker has three investors who have received five winning hot stock tips in a row from this brilliant broker and his analysts. The broker then asks the investors to make a substantial portfolio commitment given his obvious expertise in the stock picking arena. And so the illusion of the expert stock picker proliferates.

The above example has many victims—not the least of which are the three remaining "winning" investors who have put their faith, and now their money, with this broker. The ninety-seven who were ultimately ignored are actually quite fortunate in the end, as they were no longer on the hit list.

While this is a hypothetical example, this type of manipulation is used in more subtle forms throughout the investment industry. Splitting the deck successfully raises money for the broker because of the undying hope most investors have to find that special person who can pick winning stocks.

IGNORANCE IS STOCK-PICKING BLISS

Another picking example that appeared in the December 9, 2002, issue of *Fortune* magazine once again contained one of those classic stock-picking headlines—"10 Stocks to Buy Now" by David Stires. The article stated:

> *We checked in with two of the best sector strategists we know, Steve Galbraith of Morgan Stanley and the Leuthold Group's founder, Steve Leuthold, to find out what industries they believe are best positioned for the year ahead. Based on their combined outlooks, we picked five: energy, health care, industrials, materials, and technology. With their help we honed in on the most attractive groups in each of the industries, such as office electronics in the technology sector. The common thread is that all of the groups we selected should benefit from what Galbraith and Leuthold see as a slowly strengthening economy. Next we scrutinized industry and company reports, cross-examined equity analysts, and grilled top-tier fund managers like value investing stars Bill Nygren of the Oakmark fund and Jim Gipson of the Clipper fund to find the best stocks in each industry.*

Listen to all the great fundamental analysis words and phrases in that excerpt—"honed in," "scrutinized," "cross-examined," "grilled," "top tier."

So how did these stocks do? Not bad, actually.

For the one-year period ending November 30, 2003, they had a combined average return of 17.15 percent. This looks pretty good when compared with the three previous losing years of stock market returns. This list also out-distanced the popular benchmark of the S&P 500 Index, which increased by 15.09 percent during this same twelve-month period. [7]

Figure 2.2

Stock	% Change
Zebra Technologies	48.48%
Xerox	39.68%
Market Return Equity Portfolio	33.41%
CSX	24.18%
Pogo Producing	22.77%
Waste Management	18.06%
S&P 500	15.09%
Pioneer Natural Res.	15.00%
Air Prod. & Chem.	10.66%
Pfizer	8.49%
DuPont	-3.84%
Johnson & Johnson	-12.01%

However, if rather than buying this group of stocks, investors had taken a structured approach that offers the broadest and deepest diversification possible (i.e., a market return approach), they would have earned 33.41 percent during this same time period.[8] On $1 million, that is a difference of $162,600 in one year. Furthermore, the standard deviation (which measures volatility or risk) of this broadly diversified Market Return Portfolio strategy would have been much lower because of the super-diversification. (Details of the Market Return Portfolio strategy appear in chapters five and six.) The chance of *Fortune*'s individual stocks excelling consistently over time versus the MRP approach is very small. Why? Simple. With MRP you can invest in practically the entire market. With only ten picks you speculate and cast your lot on their futures alone.

MARKET ANALYST VERSUS WEATHERMAN

You may still remember watching the local weather report on one of the three channels of your black and white television. Often the gimmick was for the weatherman to come out dressed in garb that coincided with the forecast. A favorite was the ill-fitting raincoat and rain hat. The old joke about predicting the weather and "If you don't like it, hang around—it'll change in an hour or so" is universal. The equipment the weathermen used then was archaic by today's Doppler radar, real-time, computerized standards, and it is a wonder that those weathermen ever forecast correctly. With all the technology, today's meteorologists still seem to be incorrect more often than we might expect.

This brings us to the financial market analyst. Each year we see the exercise when all the financial publications and talk shows get the "expert predictions" on how the market will perform. This process also begs the question: Is there anyone who can be so wrong so often and still hold on to a job? And not just any job—one that is well-respected and highly compensated! Today's meteorologist looks downright psychic compared to the stock market analyst. Incredibly however, investors seem to overlook poor financial forecasting as if it never happened.

What short memories investors have! They seem always to be hoping to find that special guru or hot stock tip that will allow their ship to finally come in. This leads to a fundamental problem—investors typically are looking for the short-term fix rather than at the long-term view of their finances. If they were thinking long-term, they would ignore the forecasts. Instead, they would buy and hold super-diversified stock portfolios for the rest of their lives—period. Why? Because there is no better way to create long-term wealth for the average investor.

Getting in and out based on market events or the analyst-guru's call of the day, week, month, or year is a failed proposition from top to bottom. Free markets work. Capitalism is the economic miracle of history. So get in and stay in. Oh, you can still watch the market prognosticator's predictions. However, you should do it for recreation and amusement, not for making important decisions about money that may ultimately affect the quality of your life for the rest of your life.

No rainstorm lasts forever. As long-term investors, we need to keep that in mind. So when it comes to predicting, give us the weatherman. His short-term forecasts are far more accurate. And his long-term predictions? Well, he says there is always fair weather ahead.

OH, THOSE ATTENTION-GRABBING HEADLINES

Another example of stock picking takes us to the grocery store checkout line, where few investors can ignore the magazine headlines that call to them like siren songs. One such headline that we've tracked since June 1999 was from *Money* magazine. The cover title was "The Best 100 Mutual Funds—The Only List You Need."[9] The June 1999 date allows us to observe the performance of these select funds at the tail end of the bull market run through the bear market of March 2000 to November 2002 and into the market recovery of 2003. Here is the "tale of the tape" from June 1999 through December 2003:[10]

2	Funds no longer exist or have been merged into other funds
21	Funds changed their name by 2004
93	Funds are actively managed
31	Funds have 12b-1 (marketing) fees
35	Funds placed advertisements in the 1999 issue of the magazine
71	Funds disappeared from the *Money* "Top 100" list by 2003
5.35 percent	The annualized average return for the five years ending December 31, 2003
59 percent	Funds that beat their five-year annualized benchmark
57 percent	Average fund turnover ratio
1.08 percent	Average fund expense ratio

As we can see, the mutual funds fared much better than the previous individual stock examples. This is witness to the greater amount of diversification that is inherent in mutual funds.

However, a closer look at the "Best 100" begs some interesting questions. Where are the two "best" funds that disappeared? Why did twenty-one funds change their names? Also, a little more than half of the funds beat their benchmark, which means almost half did not. It was basically a coin flip. The overwhelming majority (93 percent) were actively managed (which is also indicated by the higher expense ratios and turnover ratios). And incredibly, seven out of ten of these funds fell off of this list within four years. We will see a little later how a Market Return Portfolio can mitigate most, if not all, of these difficulties.

Curiously, *Money* magazine created a new list in early 2005 containing only fifty funds. Perhaps they had grown tired of the year-to-year comparison of their "Best 100" picks and wanted to temporarily put to rest the "apples to apples" scrutiny.

We must concede that these media examples were chosen to make a point concerning stock picking in general. Furthermore, we realize that there are possibly other publications that recommended winners during these very same time periods. That said, however, consider this: With all the various opportunities to get advice from the media, which sources should investors use? Even if we assume that most of the pickers did provide good selections in the short run (and that is an enormous assumption!), we have seen no evidence that they can do it for extended periods of time—the way investors need them to. Additionally, if capital market returns are available without taking the risk of selecting the right picker, as we will soon reassert, then why take the unnecessary risk?

A further concern is that information of this nature offered in a publication does not address personal issues relating to tax brackets, liquidity needs, family situations, and the like. This speaks to the problem with interpreting mass media information as individualized advice. Unfortunately, most investors do not stop to consider this aspect.

PICKING MUTUAL FUNDS

Figure 2.3 shows the frustrating task investors often face when choosing mutual funds based on ranking services.[11]

Figure 2.3

	Fund A	Fund B	Fund C	Fund D
*Morningstar**	★★★★★	★★	★★★	★★★★
Forbes	C	A	A+	D
US News & World Report†	34	50	10	93
Wall Street Journal	E	C	A	B
Business Week	A	No Rating	B+	C

Source: **Dimensional Fund Advisors**

*Five stars is highest rating, one star is lowest rating
†100 is highest rating, 1 is lowest

Observe that these are all respected rating services. The companies employ bright people trying to apply their skills to rating funds for investors. But note the disparity among the rankings of these actual funds.

Morningstar and *Business Week* loved Fund A. The other three (*US News* in particular) did not like it at all. Fund B was a favorite of *Forbes* but evidently did not impress anyone else. Fund C was also liked by the analysts at *Forbes* and the *Wall Street Journal* but no one else (*US News* apparently hated it!). Fund D was ranked high by *Morningstar* and *US News*, but the others rated it as average at best.

According to this information, which of these funds should investors add to their portfolios?

Obviously, this diversity of opinions presents a problem for investors who are relying on the "experts" to help them make selections. We are confident that hard-working, intelligent analysts are making these judgments. The trouble is they are all using different criteria to make their assessments. So now, rather than just taking their word for it, investors are forced to judge who is using the best criteria in their rating methodologies. Who among us is qualified to undertake this task?

We would submit that we could take almost any fund in the mutual fund universe and find a similar variety of opinions. This situation as it exists is indeed frustrating for those seeking help. Unfortunately, often-times investors simply take the word of only one organization's ratings and move on. This can leave their portfolios quite vulnerable. The over-whelming majority of mutual fund investors (and their advisors) make their decisions based on this type of confusing ratings information. But there is a better way. Stay tuned.

DO YOU ENJOY THOSE SUPER BOWL COMMERCIALS?

One of the most enjoyable aspects of the Super Bowl for many people is the fierce competition among commercials. Who can forget the herding cats, Michael Jordan playing "horse" off of tall buildings with Larry Bird, or the historic 1984 commercial by Apple Computer? Each year the ads seem to get funnier, more clever, and certainly more expensive. The ticket price for the game has climbed from $10 for Super Bowl I in 1967 to $500 for Super Bowl XXXIX in 2005. Likewise, a thirty-second commercial in 2005 had an estimated cost of an incredible $2.4 million.

Well, this is fine unless you see your mutual fund company run an ad. If you do, hopefully it will be entertaining, because you just unwittingly helped pay for the most expensive thirty seconds in television. Those advertising costs are passed through to shareholders—that means you. Worst of all, this expense does little or nothing to benefit current shareholders but rather benefits the fund company's effort to recruit new customers. So enjoy the game. But afterward you might make a note to check on your mutual fund expense ratios.

THE HIGH COST OF PICKING

The *Wall Street Journal* reported in November 2003 that the average expense ratio for actively managed stock mutual funds had risen to 1.59 percent.[12] This was up from 1.54 percent the prior year. In spite of all the mutual fund scandals and huge fines that were levied against fund families, the average held steady at 1.58 percent in January 2005.[13] Costs considered in the expense ratio can include office space, staff, custody fees, legal fees, advertising, shareholder servicing, and distribution fees. Although costs vary, some researchers have estimated that marketing expenditures constitute more than half of all mutual fund expenses. This compares with using a market return strategy where the average fund expense ratio could be less than 0.40 percent.[14]

If that were the only comparison, it would be bad enough. However, there are other costs associated with stock picking and active management that are not always easy to understand. For example, trading costs typically are not included in the expense ratio, although they may be buried somewhere within the prospectus. Incredibly, some funds can even have brokerage commissions as large as their expense ratios. One estimate puts the average stock fund portfolio transaction costs at around 75 basis points, or three-quarters of 1 percent of assets.[15] Oftentimes, payments termed soft-dollar arrangements provide payments to mutual fund sellers resulting in increased commissions. Trading costs and soft dollars can erode the performance investors ultimately receive.

Another menacing return-stealing culprit is the bid-ask spread. Stocks have an ask price, which is the purchase price, and a bid, or sales price. The difference between these two is known as the spread. Foreign and small cap funds have a typical spread of 1 percent to 4 percent, but the spread may reach into the 10 percent range because these are more difficult to trade. Large company stock spreads can be as low as 0.3 percent, but may exceed 1 percent as well. Investors or fund managers that trade often in an effort to time and pick the market will feel the negative effects of the bid-ask spread to a greater degree. Add all this to the mix, and expenses—stated or not—can soar.

One additional consideration involves the objectives of the fund managers. When you have a clear understanding of their goals, then you can easily understand why the total cost of active management is so onerous. When new money for a fund is raised via good short-term performance, it leads to a bonus or a raise in salary for managers.

Funds that perform poorly do not raise as much money and are eventually phased out along with their performance records (more on this later). The managers of these poor funds may try to make up ground by changing the composition of their holdings, which can get very expensive for the shareholders as we just discussed. Ultimately, these high costs are a result of what we call misaligned interests. That is, the investors/shareholders and the investment product providers and fund managers do not share the same objectives. We will deal with these misaligned interests in more detail in chapter 4.

WHY STOCK PICKING DOESN'T WORK

1. **Choice conflict.** This is not hard to understand. How many times have you been in a restaurant and had fifty choices on the menu? Don't you tend to select the same meal over and over again at a particular eating establishment because the choice is comfortable? When given too many choices, we tend to fall back into a comfort zone and go with something familiar or make no choice at all. Stock pickers do the same. They tend to gravitate to familiar names that have been around. They follow the crowd, and this rarely offers a superior return. Fund managers who do this tend to fall into the same trap. We know this because their funds look much like each other and create overlap.

2. **Overconfidence.** Hindsight bias is lethal in the speculation world. As humans, we all tend to look at the past and say to ourselves, "I knew that was a good stock." We then fool ourselves into thinking we should be able to pick the next one correctly. Or perhaps we get a few correct and believe that stock picking is an easy trade to master. One of the most dangerous things that can ever happen to a stock picker is early success. This overconfidence is a very common financial behavior characteristic. And it can be devastating.

3. **Who is right?** Analysts watch each other. Stock trading is much like any other business where individuals are trying to stand out with some hot recommendation. They know that investors

have extremely short memories and therefore will tend to forget the bad selections as long as hope is restored with an occasional winner. Just take a look at financial magazine sales. They would not print the best-picks lists if consumers did not buy them. Unfortunately, only a few of these opinions can be right at any one time. As a stock picker, or manager, it is an almost impossible task to be right very often. Therefore, to whom do we listen?

4. **Corporate malfeasance.** Dubious accounting methods and illegal conduct by corporate executives adversely affects companies and markets. Enron is the poster child for this type of problem. How did so many analysts (basically all of them) miss this one? While this type of conduct has most likely always been present to some degree, in recent years we have seen an increase in the frequency of citations and indictments. This may be in part due to the gluttonous excess brought on by the good times of the bull market followed by the bear market of 2000 to 2002. In other words, the tide went back out and many were caught swimming naked. Therefore, even if investors could gain an advantage with the very best analysis and due diligence, the investment can end up a disaster because of one human indiscretion.

5. **Efficient markets.** We cannot get away from this reality. The fact remains that for a picker to find a security that has somehow flown below the radar of the thousands of market analysts and landed in our own little portfolio—or that of our active fund manager—it can most likely be attributed to random dumb luck rather than skill. And to think that an entire fleet could be found on a consistent basis is nonsensical to any right-minded person.

SUMMARY

The obvious question we must ask at this point is: "Why do stock pickers do it?" Investment professionals who propose stock picking as a winning strategy are generally very bright people. Some may not have been exposed to the data that discredit their methods and are honestly trying to do what is in the best interest of investors. It is also likely, however, that many of them are well aware of the data but are so entangled in the system that provides their livelihood that they do not feel they can leave it. Propping up active management is a personal financial decision for many advisors—not one made in the best interests of their clients. In other words, they must give the illusion that they are doing something (timing and/or picking) to earn their keep, rather than seeking the best strategy for their clients. Others simply pick stocks because of ego. They genuinely like to play the game with other peoples' money. Unfortunately, the financial services world is replete with conflicts of interest such as these.

In conclusion, investing in a manner that will accomplish broad capital market returns is highly preferable in the long run to a speculative, active management strategy that attempts to pick winners.

3 Chapter
Chasing Returns

Market timing and stock picking are the unhealthy habits that lead to an insidious investing disease known as chasing returns. At the root of this malady is the hope and belief that higher returns can be caught by using these failed methodologies. But chasing higher returns is an almost sure road to investment failure. Good performance tends to disappear about the time the investor arrives. Chasing returns will result in consistently buying high and selling low—the exact opposite of any investor's objective.

Consider the following story to illustrate the concept:

On January 1, 1927, Fae Future had $1 to invest any way she chose. Having been born with the ability to tell the future, she naturally chose the correct place to put her money. Fae was able to do this very same thing for the next seventy-seven years. That is, at the beginning of each year, she would invest her accumulated portfolio totally in the asset class that would be the winner with the highest return.

It is no surprise that rarely did one asset class have a long string of superiority. In fact, only once did one asset class have the highest return for four years in a row. None had it three years in a row. On ten occasions the best asset class had a two-year run. At any rate, Fae was about as successful as one can possibly be as an investor.

Consequently, Fae Future's $1 grew to approximately $817,000,000 by January 1, 2004.

On December 31, 1927, Paul Past also had $1 available to invest any way he chose. Unfortunately, Paul was not blessed with the same psychic abilities as Fae. He had to look back at the previous year's results and choose the asset class he felt was the best moving forward. Not surprising, Paul always chose the asset class that had just finished the year with the highest return (Fae's choice twelve months earlier). How much did this hindsight approach net Paul at the end of the seventy-seven years?

A whopping $1,532.

Remember, Paul did not invest in the worst asset class each year—he chose the asset class that had the best return the year before. He also had the benefit of the eleven occasions when Fae's selection had multiple-year runs as mentioned. This means he was also in the best investment of the year for thirteen of the seventy-seven years.[1]

This scenario is a microcosm of the return-chasing game investors experience in every generation. Investors hope to be Fae Future. Yet knowing this is impossible, most investors make portfolio decisions just like Paul Past.

LOSING THEIR FAIR SHARE

Studies have shown that investors will receive, on average, less than half the market return on their portfolios. The following diagram shows the profound negative effect that higher fees and the methodologies of active management (timing and picking) have on performance. During the period from 1982 to 2002, the S&P 500 Index had an annual rate of return of 13.1 percent compared with 10 percent in the average equity mutual fund. This resulted in the growth of $1 to $11.50 and $6.70, respectively. The average fund investor, according to estimates, earned only about 2.0 percent per year. This results in a minimal 50-cent profit over the twenty years.

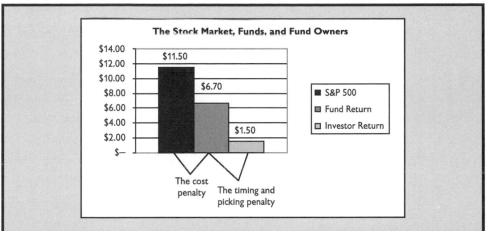

Source: **Bogle Financial Markets Research Center**

These bad results are compounded further when inflation and income taxes are taken into account. How can this be? The answer is simple: the high cost of active management and chasing returns.

The endemic nature of this chasing ailment in America makes it a critical topic to thresh out. Media hot lists are so prevalent because financial editors and program directors are aware of the addiction investors have for predicting outcomes. It should be expected that speculation in the securities market is rife with the get-rich-quick mentality. After all, in similar fields of speculation, such as horse racing and other sports betting, the mindset is the same. People want to win big by predicting outcomes.

The trouble is, in the investing world, the media and Wall Street are so highly skilled at feeding this desire through active marketing that success in the active management realm appears to be reality. Trust us when we say this is not reality. If it were, this book would not have been written. Rather we would long ago have been reclining on the beach with our Fae Future newsletter in tow.

THE CULTURE OF PERFORMANCE

Former chairman of the Securities and Exchange Commission Arthur Levitt refers to the aggressive mutual fund advertising of past returns as a part of the "culture of performance."[2] This suggests a systemic problem that is not easily overcome. Performance is nearly every investor's first criteria. Investment product vendors, knowing this, spare no expense in their advertising campaigns. They know as well as anyone that past performance is no indicator of future results, which is precisely why such a disclaimer is required on any piece of investment sales literature. However, they are in a very competitive business. Their job security and any promotions hinge on the constant attracting of new dollars to their funds. When good performance is not there to advertise, the easiest course of action is often to close the fund and move on. This leads to a discussion of another of Wall Street's games known as fund incubation.

The incubator fund strategy works something like this: A fund company opens up several new funds, each with an appealing strategy. They may rely heavily on market timing, data mining, or the next fair-haired manager with the golden touch. After each investment strategy runs its course, odds are one or two funds have hit a random hot streak and shown impressive one-year returns. These survivors can now be marketed and promoted for their high performance. The money then starts flowing in. After large amounts have been gathered, the high-risk issues are dropped and replaced with lower-risk stock positions. This technique can eventually result in creating a closet index fund that maintains reasonable performance. Sound a bit fishy? That's because it is.

These incubator funds also present investors with higher internal fund expenses due to higher advertising costs and frequent trading in an effort to find the supposed winners and attract new money. This lab experiment ends up bulldozing investors.

The incubation of funds is another indication that managers do not practice what they preach, but simply are seeking to feed the return-chasing desires of the general public. This focus on short-term results is rarely spelled out in the prospectus, per se. They will tout long-term investing and then trade frequently, searching for the right security mix for their funds. Numerous studies have shown that higher turnover in funds generally leads to below-average performance because of higher expenses.[3] Timing strategies also exacerbate this problem as they try to predict up and down market moves.

All this trading and timing results in higher costs passed on to the investor. And for what? So the fund company can generate more revenue at fund-holder expense. This is a plain example of the misaligned interests that exist between Wall Street and individual investors.

INVESTING FOR DUMMIES: AN INCUBATOR EXPERIMENT

In our never-ending quest for definitive answers, our crack investment research team put together what turned out to be a phenomenal methodology for picking winning stocks in January 2004. As a result of this research, we created a hypothetical mutual fund family—the DUMB (Diversified United States Mutual Fund Balderdash) State Funds. Rather than waste time with fundamental analysis or stock charting, we simply created a single criterion that would have allowed us to beat every actively managed fund in the *Morningstar* universe of funds.

This painstaking research was hashed out in about ten minutes. We simply divided all of the stocks on the US exchanges into state categories. The companies were placed into mutual funds based on their corporate headquarters' location. Naturally, we ended up with fifty funds in our incubator grouping. The winner turned out to be the Wyoming Fund, which we affectionately renamed the Cowboy State Fund. This fund had an incredible one-year performance of 168.2 percent for the calendar year 2003. This was good enough to have beaten every one of the 2,121 actively managed US mutual funds[4] with their sophisticated timing and picking strategies. These results would have allowed us to blow our own horn and advertise our tremendous results in every major media forum in the country and gather piles of investor dollars.

DUMB State Family of Funds 2003

Rank	Fund	1 Yr Total Return	Rank	Fund	1 Yr Total Return
1	Wyoming	168.22%	26	Michigan	64.10%
2	Oklahoma	156.79%	27	Nevada	61.84%
3	Arizona	147.15%	28	Louisiana	60.93%
4	Colorado	145.18%	29	Connecticut	60.81%
5	Utah	140.44%	30	North Dakota	60.65%
6	Washington	118.33%	31	New Hampshire	59.53%
7	California	109.83%	32	Pennsylvania	59.04%
8	Massachusetts	106.61%	33	Maine	58.81%
9	Georgia	103.73%	34	Arkansas	56.90%
10	Florida	103.41%	35	Iowa	55.50%
11	Minnesota	99.78%	36	Alabama	55.36%
12	Oregon	91.87%	37	Tennessee	50.69%
13	New York	90.48%	38	Wisconsin	48.89%
14	Alaska	87.02%	39	Delaware	47.92%
15	North Carolina	86.37%	40	Nebraska	47.83%
16	Idaho	86.21%	41	Indiana	45.93%
17	New Jersey	84.17%	42	Kansas	45.66%
18	Texas	83.27%	43	West Virginia	45.30%
19	Mississippi	78.40%	44	South Carolina	43.92%
20	Hawaii	77.73%	45	Ohio	43.78%
21	Illinois	71.63%	46	New Mexico	42.91%
22	Maryland	69.73%	47	Missouri	41.15%
23	Virginia	66.37%	48	Montana	30.07%
24	Rhode Island	65.99%	49	South Dakota	29.54%
25	Kentucky	65.93%	50	Vermont	22.21%

What does this exercise tell us? First of all, if you see a real active manager with superior results in the short run, it is quite likely to be plain dumb luck or the result of an incubator type strategy. Second, this exercise shows how one ridiculously simple and random criterion can outperform the best-funded investment management teams available. Third, the fact that we used only a one-year time frame gave it little credibility. It was no surprise that the Cowboy State Fund dropped to near the bottom of the heap to forty-third place in 2004. It followed a typical short-lived pattern of mutual funds that use stock picking and/or timing techniques to achieve temporary success.

The Nevada Fund climbed into first place on the 2004 list after finishing twenty-seventh in 2003. This means that in order to pick it as the 2004 winner you would have had to ignore the twenty-six funds in front of it in 2003.

As crazy and thoughtless as this approach sounds, we concluded we had a proprietary idea—dumb as it was. Believe it or not, we found out after the fact that this approach is actually being used already. There are mutual funds that actually do invest only in companies of one particular state as part of their unique strategy.

P.S. This is a tongue-in-cheek example. The Nevada Fund does not actually exist. Sorry. We know you return chasers are disappointed.

HIDING THE BAD EGGS

Another area that is little publicized in the active management world is that of survivorship bias, which occurs when mutual funds fail to perform and are swept under the rug like so many dust bunnies. This can be a by-product of fund incubation or just plain bad performance. At press time, there were 16,842 mutual funds in the *Morningstar* database.[5] According to the *Wall Street Journal* in March 2004, mutual funds continued to close and/or merge at an astonishing rate in the previous three years. They reported that 4,117 funds were either merged into other funds or closed in the combined years of 2001–2003.[6] This eliminated more than 4,000 track records that were most likely below average. When these track records are purged, the average returns on all remaining funds go up—thus skewing the average and creating the survivorship bias.

Incredibly, during this same three-year period, an additional 6,161 new funds were created. This mutual fund shell game makes it more difficult to get accurate performance information. So beware of vanishing funds and the survivorship bias their demise causes.

FIRST TO WORST

The chart below shows the results of the top ten US equity funds in two four-year time periods, back to back.[7]

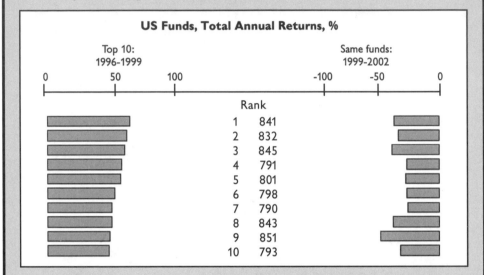

US Funds, Total Annual Returns, %

Top 10: 1996-1999

Same funds: 1999-2002

Rank		
1	841	
2	832	
3	845	
4	791	
5	801	
6	798	
7	790	
8	843	
9	851	
10	793	

Source: **Bogle Financial Markets Research Center**

The results clearly show how fickle funds can be in different time periods. As the chart shows, the top ten funds returned between 45 percent and 65 percent from 1996 through 1999. These are impressive results that would catch the attention of any investor. Imagine owning a portfolio of funds with this type of performance.

Unfortunately, the same ten funds did a complete turnaround as they all plummeted to the bottom of the pack in the next four-year period (in fact, fund No. 9 became the absolute worst performer). This is your worst nightmare if you are a return chaser. Yet it would be hard to find an investor, or even a broker, who would fault a decision to buy these funds in January 1999 based on those results. This is because of the extreme allure that often envelops overambitious investors.

Chasing these returns would have been devastating to any portfolio. Similarly, chasing any returns is likely to be detrimental to a long-term investing objective.

CHASING MUTUAL FUNDS

Figures 3.1 and 3.2 illustrate what can occur when timing, picking, and chasing returns collide.

Assume we have two mutual funds or money managers—A and B. On day one, $100,000 is invested in each fund. At the end of year one, we see that fund B has performed much better, with a balance of $140,000 (Figure 3.1). What is the emotional return-chasing move an investor may make? Naturally it is to move all the money into fund B. The next year, we see a disappointing result with B as it loses 10 percent. The consummate chaser is depicted in Figure 3.2. He would have moved the fund B balance of $225,000 back to fund A. If this chasing pattern continued for the duration of the five years, the end result would be that the original $200,000 portfolio would have shrunk to $190,575 (Figure 3.2). That is a geometric return of minus 0.96 percent. Staying the course in both funds, as shown in Figure 3.1, would have provided a combined average return of 8.31 percent and a total of $298,864 at the end of the period. That represents more than 50 percent more dollars in the account!

Figure 3.1

Fund A	Year 1	Year 2	Year 3	Year 4	Year 5	Avg. Return	Geometric Return
Return	10%	10%	10%	10%	10%	10.00%	10.00%
Balance	$110,000	$121,000	$133,100	$146,410	$161,051		
Fund B	Year 1	Year 2	Year 3	Year 4	Year 5	Avg. Return	Geometric Return
Return	40%	-10%	25%	-30%	25%	10.00%	6.62%
Balance	$140,000	$126,000	$157,500	$110,250	$137,813		

Figure 3.2

Fund A	Year 1	Year 2	Year 3	Year 4	Year 5	Avg. Return	Geometric Return
Portfolio Value	$110,000	$-	$247,500	$-	$190,575	1.00%	-0.96%
Fund B	Year 1	Year 2	Year 3	Year 4	Year 5	Avg. Return	Geometric Return
Portfolio Value	$140,000	$225,000	$-	$173,250	$-		

In addition to providing evidence that chasing does not work, this table also shows the importance of reducing volatility or portfolio fluctuations whenever possible. The arithmetic average for both funds in Figure 3.1 is 10 percent. However, the geometric return is 3.38 percent lower in the more volatile fund B (6.62 percent versus 10 percent). Thus the actual dollars in fund B is $23,238 less than fund A.

Note that these examples look at only five years. As we will discuss in detail in chapter 5, all portfolios are long-term in nature with limited exceptions. Therefore imagine the difference in dollars over twenty, thirty, or forty years with unwarranted volatility or return-chasing dragging the balance down.

HIRING THE BEST?

There is a fallacy in thinking among return-chasing investors. They want to fire their money or fund managers after a bad year and hire one that has just had a good year. They tend to treat their portfolios as if they owned a pro sports franchise. Firing head coaches in an effort to find that guru who will take them to the championship is a matter of course in the sports world.[8]

It is the same in the investment world, only different. First of all, it's the same in that investors feel that by hiring the best money manager based on last "season," they can buy a winner. It is different in that head coaches actually do have direct influence on their players—money managers have no influence on the securities markets whatsoever.

By continually firing and hiring money managers, an investor is unwittingly firing a manager when a fund is down and hiring another when a fund is up. Does this sound right? Buying high and selling low? This is definitely not a game plan for investment success. Furthermore, it represents just one more pitfall associated with active portfolio management.

FUNDS PROSPER, INVESTORS CHASE

Figure 3.3 shows the inverse relationship between the assets that are gathered from investors and the performance over a twenty-five-year period in an actual US large cap fund.[9]

Figure 3.3

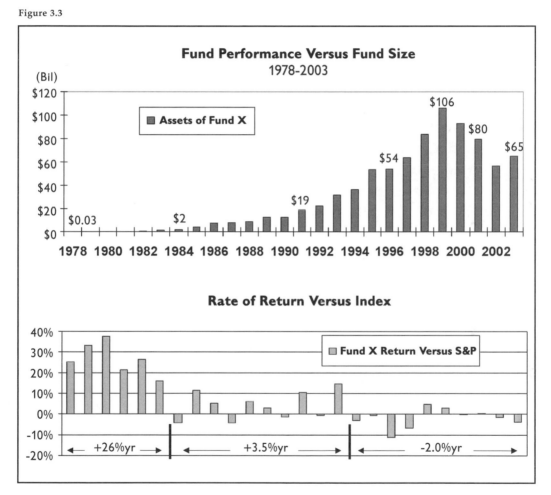

Source: Bogle Financial Markets Research Center

The charts clearly show that by the time investors realize the advertised returns are no longer present, years have passed and many dollars and opportunities have been lost. This is a clear indication of how the return-chasing mentality of investors can be preyed upon by the mutual fund industry.

TACTICAL ALLOCATION

Evidence that timing, picking, and chasing do not work has been more broadly accepted by some concerning individual stock positions. However, a form of chasing is still embraced by many—including most investment advisors. Known as tactical asset allocation, this is the idea that specific asset class allocations can be timed.

Tactical asset allocation involves surveying the landscape on a macro-economic level in order to determine the best place to invest at the moment. Shifting all or a part of a portfolio from small to large US companies or from international value to growth categories are examples. While this concept certainly can be couched in a way that appears to reflect much consideration and planning, it still smacks of timing. Additionally, if timing is present, picking and chasing are almost always involved as well.

A strategic allocation that ignores broad market indicators and is based on needs unique to each investor's written financial plan remains the prudent course of action. This includes the consideration of risk preference, cash flow needs, health issues, and family situations (among other things). Once analyzed, these should be used to create an investment policy statement (IPS) that outlines the proper allocation strategy. If a change in a personal situation occurs, the allocation may then warrant a review and possible adjustment. Otherwise, the IPS will help prevent potentially harmful ad hoc revisions to a long-term investment game plan. This is a very effective way to avoid the temptations that active management places in front of investors who might be tempted to employ any tactical allocation techniques.

BORROWING TROUBLE

Active portfolio management with its timing, picking, and return-chasing activity ultimately will provide plenty of trouble for its disciples. In some cases, the extreme desire to win in the securities lottery will create far more trouble than one can even imagine.

Take homemaking icon Martha Stewart. She dominated headlines as she struggled for acquittal in her stock trading case from 2002 through 2004. Stewart was not charged with insider trading. Technically, she was not an insider because she was not employed by the company whose stock was in question. However, she was charged with wrongdoing concerning a stock trade.

It is astounding to contemplate the negative effect this incident had on Stewart's fortune. In comparison to the wealth she had before the event (easily in the nine- or ten-digit range), this five-figure transaction seems insignificant. Yet, this overwhelming desire to get an edge in the securities markets through active trading is common among investors at all levels. This scenario is even more remarkable when it is considered that Stewart once had a career as a stockbroker.

Situations like this can be easily avoided when investors employ a structured market return approach to portfolio management. To put it another way, you should be an investor instead of a speculator.

The practices of active management can promote emotional behavior that is a danger to all investors. It is truly amazing to see the power of picking and timing, when even those trained in the securities business cannot escape its allure.

THE BIGGEST EXPENSE
IS ACTIVE MANAGEMENT

In chapter 2 we discussed just how high mutual fund expense ratios have climbed. However, the highest expense by far an investor will ever incur comes from using active management.

Morningstar data indicate that the average turnover ratio for actively managed domestic stock funds exceeded 97 percent in 2004.[10] This means that if there were one hundred stock positions at the beginning of the year, nearly all of them would have changed by the end of the year. This level of trading not only creates high hard-dollar costs, it is also a sure indicator that a manager is picking and timing.

The chances are minute that active management can provide any value to a long-term portfolio. Investors that do not understand this are stuck with the bill. This bill, generated by active management, is the biggest expense of all to investors, as they time, pick, and chase returns on their way to inferior performance.

WHY CHASING RETURNS DOESN'T WORK

1. **Randomness.** Active managers seek to achieve success in a system that is by nature random. Another way to put it: Return chasers depend on plain dumb luck. And any gambler knows that good luck is hit and miss. Achieving good fortune consistently is not possible in a system that intrinsically cannot provide it.

2. **Timing.** Whether it is a rabbit, a baseball, or a common cold, in order to catch something, timing is everything. As we have seen, timing the market is futile because of human shortcomings.

3. **The system is self-serving.** The active marketing employed by the investment industry is counterproductive because it entices investors into buying its best-performing products of yesterday. These misaligned interests bring its purveyors profits, while investors usually get only heartache and failure.

SUMMARY

The evidence presented concerning active management is sufficient to create serious misgivings about a flawed system. Investors who continue to apply active management methods adhere to Albert Einstein's famous definition of insanity: doing the same thing over and over again and expecting different results.[11] The results cannot be different as long as the ineffective methods of timing, picking, and return chasing are used.

Henry Blodget, a former Internet stock analyst and Wall Street insider himself, even goes so far as to suggest that actively managed mutual funds should post prominently on their Web sites cigarette pack-style warning labels that read: "Active management is hazardous to your wealth." [12]

The first three chapters of this book were designed to give investors a synopsis of why active management, at its foundation, is a failure. This popular system, which promotes emotional behavior, is a danger to all investors. We believe far more money has been lost because of this culprit than all the accounting and trading scandals combined throughout history. At the heart of the matter is the continued systematic training of Wall Street representatives who propagate a failed philosophy, dooming their clients to investment returns well below what the market offers freely.

In spite of the Wall Street juggernaut, we remain steadfast in our goal to educate as many willing listeners as possible to the proper way to invest. The upcoming solution section of the book, "Creating Wealth Without Worry," will do just that.

PART II:
CREATING WEALTH
WITHOUT WORRY

All truths are easy to understand once they are discovered; the point is to discover them.

–Galileo Galilei

4 Chapter
The Financial Services Industry

As we begin the solution section of the book, we want to offer some insight into the financial services industry.

The headlines in recent years make it clear that the financial services industry is experiencing many difficult challenges. Scandals involving corporate governance, mutual fund trading, and investment research analysts have made investors increasingly cynical. And well they should be. These shortcomings exemplify the system's flawed nature. While a protracted discussion of these issues may be interesting to some, we prefer to deal with these issues as they concern individual investors. Therefore, we will examine the industry as it currently exists at the user level. In other words, at the system's point of entry—the investment advisor.

Investors are familiar with the traditional brokerage system that has been in place for many years. This system has been the bastion of active management techniques. The Wall Street goliaths of the industry have dominated the marketplace with overwhelming media power and lobbying abilities for decades. The situation has become especially confusing as these old-line wire houses joined the fee advice bandwagon in the 1990s. Many brokers now offer fee-based investment advice along with commission-based products.

This change in the stockbroker world, along with other changes, makes it difficult to determine the difference between one financial service professional and another. There has been a commingling of core competencies that confuses the general public. The fact that nearly all the representatives working in the industry now call themselves "financial advisors" adds to the mystification.

In times past, bankers were bankers, insurance agents sold policies, brokers sold securities, and CPAs gave tax advice. This was the environment for decades because of longstanding federal securities laws enacted largely in response to the stock market crash of 1929.[1] This legislation separated the industry players. But to a large degree, these legal barriers have been removed in recent years. Consequently, everyone is in one another's back yard. This despecialization and dilution of services can be detrimental to individual investors.

FIDUCIARY ADVISORS VERSUS BROKER FACILITATORS

The crucial issue that must be addressed when seeking professional financial advice is the role that the advisors are willing to take in the relationship. Are they willing to act in the manner of a fiduciary?

Most brokers and financial representatives are regulated by the National Association of Securities Dealers (NASD) and must simply adhere to a rule widely referred to as the suitability rule, which requires that brokers make a reasonable effort to gain appropriate financial information from a client before making specific investment recommendations.

A fiduciary, by contrast, is generally defined as an individual or organization that has a special relationship with the duty toward another individual or organization to act in the highest good faith and with integrity.[2] Arthur Levitt, former chairman of the Securities and Exchange Commission, defines a fiduciary as an "individual entrusted with investment decisions on behalf of another who is obligated to make decisions in the client's best interest."[3] For the purposes of our discussion, we will consider fiduciaries to be those willing to act in the best interests of their clients and to disclose any real or implied conflicts of interest.

A fiduciary standard is generally considered more stringent and broader than the NASD suitable sale standard. With this in mind, what investor would not rather have the more strict parameters in the relationship provided by a fiduciary? Clearly, removing conflicts of interests—what we call misaligned interests—will better ensure that the advisor is offering objective advice.

There remains a line—although blurry—between most financial service representatives and fiduciary advisors. We take the position that once an advisor has held himself out as an expert and a particular financial strategy has been recommended, the relationship should be considered fiduciary in nature. But regardless of whether brokers or advisors actually are fiduciaries in a legal sense is still largely an issue for the courts to one day decide.

Because the words "broker," "representative," and "advisor" often are considered interchangeable, too many investors fail to realize that many in the financial services industry, in spite of their titles, are basically sales people. As representatives of investment product manufacturers, they may be more loyal to their employers or suppliers than to their clients. This arrangement also tends to make them more likely to become order takers or facilitators for financial product vendors rather than true financial advisors. This divided loyalty begs the question: whom do you want investing your money? You should be your advisor's only focus.

Advisors who are willing to act in a fiduciary manner give their first loyalty to the client. The client pays the advisor directly. There are no soft-dollar arrangements. There are no bonuses or trips to the Caribbean for selling certain products. There is no Big Brother looking over the representative's shoulder and influencing his or her objectivity.

This direct-pay fee arrangement greatly increases the chances that the advisor and client will have their interests in alignment. Furthermore, the direct-pay system better allows the client to quantify the true value of the relationship. Think about it. How do you know the true value of something when you cannot accurately ascertain its cost? Direct pay alleviates concerns over the hidden charges that so frustrate investors.

The remainder of this chapter is designed to equip you with the knowledge and questions you need to ask when interviewing and engaging the proper type of investment advisor.

ACTIVE MARKETING

Forget active management and its failed methodologies. What Wall Street firms actually do excel at is making investors believe that they have what is best for clients. We've coined a phrase for this—we call it active marketing.

Part of this marketing shrewdness involves appearing all-knowing regardless of the market's direction. As brilliant marketers, those involved in active marketing are always in a position to develop new products that will be the answer. Their advice seems to shift as quickly as the wind as they are always at the ready with newfangled solutions. Unfortunately, most of these solutions are more beneficial to the product manufacturers and representatives than the clients they are intended to serve. Once again, we see the misaligned interests between the client and the investment firm.

Active marketing is common when it comes to proprietary products. Financial product manufacturers naturally will promote their own offerings to their representatives. This concept is not difficult to understand. When we go to a Chevrolet dealership and see the Chevrolet logo on the salesman's shirt pocket, we expect him to sell us a Chevrolet. He is not going to spend time comparing his vehicles to a Ford or Lexus unless he has a clear advantage. Rather, he will dwell on the positive attributes of the dealer's automobiles. It's no surprise then, that proprietary financial products end up as the recommendation all too often, even though the representative may claim to be objective.

Proprietary investment products are especially prevalent in the areas of mutual funds, variable annuities, and variable life insurance. Proprietary offerings tend to be more profitable to product manufacturers because they are able to cut out the middleman and distribute through their own corps of representatives. These products may have surrender charges that can last as long as twelve years. This could mean that long after the product has stopped performing and the brokers have been paid their commission, the client is stuck. In addition, proprietary offerings tend to have higher expenses.

A successful portfolio can be built without using these products. By ignoring the Wall Street promotional juggernaut, investors do themselves an enormous long-term investing favor. Stay away from not only active management but also active marketing.

ALPHABET SOUP CREDENTIALS

What do these mean? CFS, CFP®, PFS, CLU, ChFC, CIC, AAMS, CIMA, CPA, CIS, CFA®, CRSP, MSFS, RIA, CMFC, CRPC. Believe it or not, these are all credentials available to financial services professionals. Small wonder that investors can get confused with this alphabet soup.

All of the designations listed above are associated with worthy educational endeavors and are, to some extent, beneficial. However, in an effort to narrow the field, we maintain that the Certified Financial Planner™ (CFP®) mark is one good qualifying denominator to consider when choosing an advisor. In the last decade, this credential has become widely accepted as the financial planning industry's highest standard. It carries a three-year experience requirement and assurance of completion of a rigorous comprehensive exam covering all aspects of financial planning including investing. It also requires continuing education on a regular basis (including ethics courses).

Another pertinent designating acronym is the RIA, or Registered Investment Advisor. This entity is registered with either the state securities department of jurisdiction or the Securities and Exchange Commission depending on the amount of investment assets under its management. An advisor acting on behalf of an RIA is an Investment Advisory Representative (IAR). A Registered Investment Advisor is set up when fee advice is given by a firm. It does not necessarily designate an independent firm giving objective advice. Most brokerage houses now have RIA arms. The RIA is a legally required entity and should not be considered a certification of objectivity.

SEVEN ESSENTIAL QUESTIONS TO ASK WHEN INTERVIEWING AN ADVISOR

Choosing the right financial advisor is a critical, potentially life-changing decision. Based on the previous description of how various entities deliver financial services, the following list of questions is designed to provide a platform from which an investor can make an informed decision:

Question 1:   **Is your firm independent?** The word "independent" can have different meanings. Therefore the answer to this question will almost always be "yes," initially. This is because any advisor knows the value the questioner perceives in an affirmative answer. The definition we are looking for in this context, however, is this: having no association with any entities that adversely affect objectivity. This list of entities could include banks, insurance companies, traditional wire (stockbroker) houses, and broker-dealers (even "independent" ones).

A truly independent firm has no association with these organizations but rather is organized simply as a Registered Investment Advisor (RIA) compensated with fees collected directly from the client. This arrangement gives the independent firm the ability to seek the best solutions for the client while minimizing the chance of a misaligned interest. This eliminates the pressure to push certain products which is often associated with parent company arrangements. The bottom line is that a representative (or, in alphabet soup terms, an IAR) of an independent Registered Investment Advisor can act in a fiduciary manner that eliminates conflicts of interest and applies the highest professional standard available to the client relationship.

Question 2:   **How are you compensated and by how much?** Financial advisors can be paid in several different ways: salary, commissions, flat project fees, hourly fees, percentage fees for assets managed, annual retainer, or a combination of any of the above. None of these compensation methods is innately bad or good. However, in being consistent with our overriding consideration, when a client is working with an advisor, a fee-based arrangement has far less chance of producing a conflict of interest. In other words, an advisor who is compensated with fees—directly from the client—is far less likely to be influenced by financial product vendors. Because the advisor is responsible only to the client for remuneration, he or she is likely to act in the best interest of the client. Therefore, make sure the name at the top of the advisor's paycheck is yours.

Amounts for hourly fees, project fees, and annual retainer arrangements can vary greatly. A comparison of two or three advisors would be a prudent course of action. Concerning the percentage charged for asset management, generally an annual amount of one percent should be the high end of any arrangement, with a reduction in the percentage charged for larger portfolios down to around 0.30 percent.

Question 3: **What is your experience, and what are your qualifications?** Vernon Law once said, "Experience is a hard teacher because she gives the test first, the lesson afterward."[4] With that said, in the important area of money, it is not a good idea to allow someone to learn with your nest egg. The financial services industry is known for being an aggressive recruiter of inexperienced sales representatives. It is a difficult profession in which to become established and most are forced to live paycheck to paycheck early in their careers. The average four-year retention of financial representatives is as low as 11 percent in some areas of the industry.[5] If a newer advisor is going to be considered, make sure the advisor has an established independent firm upon whose experience he or she can draw.

In addition to the minimum requirements discussed, seeking advisors who work specifically with people in your situation is very beneficial. There are many advisors who accept any client who successfully fogs a mirror, particularly when they are getting started in their careers. Ask for demographic data on the clientele of an advisory firm so you can see the firm's representatives are accustomed to working with individuals with your similar needs, objectives, and problems. (If you need brain surgery, it is not wise to use a heart surgeon to perform the operation—brilliant as the heart surgeon may be.)

WHAT ABOUT ASKING FOR REFERRALS?

It is a natural tendency to want to visit with current clients of an advisory firm to get an idea of their level of satisfaction. Therefore, to ask for one or two referrals may be a good idea. Unfortunately, in the world we live in, confidentiality laws may delay this process as the advisor will probably want to get permission from the current client before such an inquiry is made. Another problem with a referral request is the likelihood that you will be referred only to the advisor's very favorite clients (or maybe even a relative), who may give you a biased view.

There is an alternative that may give a more comprehensive view of the firm. Any reputable firm looking to improve service should be asking for evaluation and feedback from its clientele on a regular basis. When interviewing potential advisors, ask them for copies of their written client survey. This survey should have been done so that the client identity is not revealed, thus allowing for candid responses. Typically, 30 to 50 percent of the clients will respond to a survey of this nature. If the firm indicates that it has one hundred clients, then you should be able to view thirty to fifty surveys. There will most likely be some negative comments on some of the surveys. After all, no one is perfect. In fact, clients may be more likely to return a survey when they have a complaint. If no negative comments exist on any of the forms, beware—you may be the victim of a scrubbing of the data. At any rate, the client survey approach can be an excellent way to get an indication of the quality of the firm you are considering.

Question 4:   What is your approach to providing financial advice?
In the past, the majority of advisors have often offered investment recommendations without having sufficient facts concerning client goals, objectives, and challenges. Any advisor worth his salt

will recommend creating a written financial plan before offering any financial or investment advice. To do otherwise is tantamount to malpractice. It is like receiving a prescription from your doctor without having been examined or diagnosed. This written financial plan can initially include a retirement cash flow analysis, an investment policy statement, and a risk management analysis. Often, an estate analysis also is warranted.

Once this written plan is completed and analyzed, the implementation should proceed with recommendations concerning various investment options and risk management tools. Obviously, any investment advice that involves active management techniques, as discussed earlier, should be summarily dismissed along with the advisor. Remember that capitalism creates wealth—not advisors. The advisor's job is to protect the capital that investors are entitled to.

This is a good subject to broach before the written plan is started. It is not prudent to have a plan created by an advisor who probably cannot implement it properly.

Question 5:   Does your firm use a team approach? A common misperception is that larger financial firms are better by mere virtue of their size. However, in most cases, large national firms are government-like bureaucracies that actually only lease space to individual representatives in their offices. While a visit to the local branch may give the impression of a team approach, it is likely to be an organization with multiple solo brokers with perhaps a shared personal assistant.

Ironically, smaller independent firms are typically better at building a team that can collectively devote their knowledge and energies to a client's best interests. We call this fiduciary organizational intelligence. As we know, two heads are better than one.

Working as a true team means that all clients are clients of the firm—not clients of individual advisors within the firm. This also helps with continuity in the event something happens to specific advisors and they are no longer part of the firm. Additionally, in smaller independent firms, the owners/principals are usually involved in the client relationship directly.

Question 6:   Will you provide in writing a description of the specific services you are recommending? Whether they are providing financial planning or asset management services, registered advisors should be prepared to provide a written sample agreement for your review in an initial meeting. This should include the delivery of a Form ADV, Part II (a document required by the Securities and Exchange Commission that provides pertinent information concerning the background and detailed operation of the firm and its principals and representatives). These documents will allow a prospective client the opportunity to compare what is said in an initial interview with what is in writing. If there is no willingness to provide such documentation, then simply walk away. This is not an advisor worth your consideration.

Question 7:   Are you willing to act in a fiduciary manner in this relationship? Because it is the central message of this chapter, we have saved this most important question for last. Most of the other questions in this list have implications concerning fiduciary responsibility. But there is no better way to get to the heart of the matter than by simply asking this question directly. Some representatives may not even completely understand the question or its implications. For reasons cited previously, this question is likely to disturb many of the brokers and representatives who do fully comprehend it. They are often in no position—either professionally or with their business entity structure—to take on the responsibility that an affirmative answer to this question demands.

No client should accept or expect anything less than the standard that is implied by an advisor being a fiduciary: to act in the best interests of the client and disclose any real or implied conflicts of interest. Once again, if a potential advisor cannot answer this question with a swift and confident "Yes!" then walk away.

BEWARE THE FREE LUNCH

We have all heard this warning a thousand times: There is no such thing as a free lunch. Yet from time to time we all fall prey to the overused sales tactic of offering something for nothing. One approach popular in the financial services world is the free financial analysis. A broker will offer to create an initial analysis of your situation at no charge. If anything appears amiss in the plan, the client can engage to have a complete plan done for a nominal fee or perhaps for no charge if the client agrees to implement the final plan with the broker. That implementation means buying financial products. The broker receives a commission, a fee, a trip to the Caribbean—you get the picture.

A conflict-free way of doing business is better for the investor. Advisors should take a look at a client's financial data in order to assess the level of planning needed to assist them. Next, the advisor should be engaged in writing to complete the written financial plan on a flat fee or hourly basis. If implementation of the plan recommendations is desired after the plan is evaluated, the client then has an opportunity to make that decision separately. The planning and implementation phases should be separate services. This way the client can receive an unbiased plan with no strings attached. That is, no obligation to invest or buy a product from the representative because of all the trouble they went to.

SUMMARY

This chapter is intended to provide a clearer understanding of the financial services delivery system at the user level. We can assure you there are financial advisory firms in your community that adhere to the standards addressed in this chapter. As a client, you should not settle for anything less than a perfect score on this list of seven questions. If an advisor gets only five or six right, move on. You deserve to have the finest help available. It is your financial well-being at stake, and choice of an advisor is a very serious decision that you must get right the first time.

In a nutshell, if you want to enhance the chances of having a successful financial advisory experience, look for a firm that:

- Is independent

- Uses a fee structure where advisors are paid directly from clients

- Uses a market return approach

- Is team oriented

- And whose advisors are

  - Experienced

  - Well-educated (preferably CFP® professionals)

  - Willing to operate in the manner of a fiduciary

Remember, this list is concrete and to be used in total. Unless the advisor and firm pass all the criteria, keep looking.

Highly successful people in every walk of life—whether business, politics, sports, or family life—have one thing in common: They surround themselves with talented and highly qualified people to assist them. But, always keep in mind that the advisor is not doing you a favor by managing your finances. The advisor is your paid employee. You are the boss. Never hire anyone but the best and most qualified candidate. Select the best the first time around.

Chapter 5
Success for All

Many of us remember watching *The Wizard of Oz* as children. We recall that moment when Dorothy and her ragtag group of traveling companions finally reach the Emerald City and stand trembling in the presence of the Wizard—that seemingly omnipotent power they have never seen or heard who holds their fate in his hands. And then, of course, we remember the disappointment. But what about that strange sense of relief we feel when the Wizard turns out to be nothing more than a nervous little man hiding behind a curtain? In the end, Dorothy learns that she had the tools to accomplish the very thing she desired all along—her ruby slippers. She then closes her eyes and chants, "There's no place like home; there's no place like home. . . ."

It's time to pull back the curtain and reveal the truth. The wizardry of Wall Street is history. As an investor, you now have the ability to achieve just what you need and desire. Free markets are the means by which you can get back home, financially speaking.

This leads us to the tenet that is the cornerstone of this entire book:

Market return is there for the taking.

When you fully appreciate this concept, it revolutionizes the way you think about investing as well as how you invest. Not only will it change your life as you no longer concern yourself with the best place to put your money, but this market return precept also allows you the opportunity to stop worrying about your financial future and live in your glorious present. Eliminating this concern allows you the time and freedom to attend to the things in life that are most important.

EVERYBODY WINS

How can we make this claim that everybody wins? Easy—we believe in the efficiency of the free market. And we're not alone in our beliefs. Great leaders such as Abraham Lincoln, Theodore Roosevelt, and Ronald Reagan all shared our faith in the people and ideals of capitalism and democracy. They knew then just as we know now that free markets work.

Capitalism, which promotes the free setting of prices based on the decisions and values of the entire economy, is the reason our current way of life prevails. There are billions of factors at work in the economy at any given time. Individuals and business entities continually make decisions all affecting the system in different ways—some positive, some negative, some indifferent. But the system works. It is a phenomenon that engenders an indomitable spirit that can be found in free markets all over the world. To prove this, one would need only to examine three of the most profound economic experiments of the last sixty years: West Germany versus East Germany, South Korea versus North Korea, and mainland China versus Hong Kong. In these examples we see a stark contrast between what government intervention in the form of regulation of prices (both for goods and markets) can do, versus the system that allows the markets to find their own way in setting prices. This lack of intervention (which ultimately drives economic growth) provides opportunities for individuals—and thus capital markets.

Will we still experience difficult markets periodically? Count on it. When? Who knows? And furthermore, who cares? As long as we have the system that allows prices to seek their own way, then economic growth will occur. With this in mind, shouldn't investors be most afraid of not being in the market when it goes to 20,000 rather than being in the market if it goes down to 2,000? In time, one is certain to happen, the other is not.

Source: NASA

	North Korea	South Korea
Population (2004)	22,697,553	48,598,175
Infant mortality (2004)	24.84 deaths/1,000 live births	7.18 deaths/1,000 live births
GDP (2003)	$29.58 billion	$857.8 billion
Electricity production (2001)	30.01 billion kWh	290.7 billion kWh
Exports (2003)	$1.044 billion f.o.b.	$201.3 billion f.o.b.
Telephones in use	1.1 million (2001)	22.877 million (2003)

Source: CIA World Factbook

THE GLOW OF FREEDOM

A picture truly is worth a thousand words. The satellite photograph above was taken at night over Southeast Asia. The white outlines show the borders of North and South Korea with Japan shining to the east.

In the North you can see the harsh reality of a society that has been devoid of the great economic opportunities that free markets offer. It is a society truly in the dark, both literally with a shortage of electricity-producing capabilities and economically as they are subdued by a regime of central economic planning via communism.

By contrast, the vibrant free market economy in the South illuminates not only the thriving cities and towns on a summer evening, but also is a shining example of what the spirit of free enterprise can accomplish in any culture that embraces it.

What more do we need to know before we invest in the economic miracle we call capitalism?

OPTIMISM—THE ONLY REALITY

Shortly after the bear market recession of 2000 through 2002, a luncheon was held with Michael Cox, senior vice president and chief economist for the Federal Reserve Bank of Dallas. Before he began his speech, he indicated that there would be a Q&A session when he finished. He stated, "Before you ask the question, let me just say that the American economy is sound. I am accused often of being an optimist. In fact, I am simply a realist. There has never been a recession that we have not come out of, and I do not expect it to be any different this time."

BULLS AND BEARS

Figure 5.1 below shows the history of United States bull and bear markets based on the S&P 500 Index over a time period of more than seven decades.

Figure 5.1

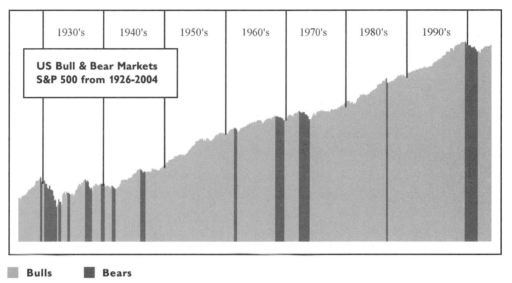

Note the duration of the bull markets versus the bear markets.[1] In total, bull markets have dominated in the United States more than 80 percent of the time. The bull runs went up a total of 3,700 percent versus the market going down a total of 451 percent during the bear cycles. Furthermore, the average gain for the fourteen bull market time periods was 264 percent. This compares with an average loss of 35 percent for the thirteen bear markets. Is it now easier to understand why investors should have absolute confidence in capital markets?

This inevitable expansion of capital markets is a windfall for all who are market return investors.

A CUB MARKET?

Periodically—quite often actually—markets will show little in the way of gains and may appear to be going sideways. For example, during the first nine months of 2004, the Dow Jones Industrial Average was down 2.09 percent and the S&P 500 Index was up only 1.53 percent. When this type of "flat" activity occurs, we see more and more headlines that imply the bull has run its course and another bear market could be in the offing.

With this in mind, we researched market patterns since 1926 and discovered a new market species that is quite interesting and reassuring. We call this new creature the "cub market." Before bears grow up, they are cubs. We define a cub as a market downturn of between 5 and 20 percent. (Once the decline reaches more than 20 percent, it grows into a bear market.)

With this new animal defined, we hunted for as many as we could find by analyzing the S&P 500 Index from 1926 through 2003. We discovered eighty-nine cub and/or bear markets during this seventy-eight-year time frame. Thirteen of the cubs grew up to become bear markets. In twenty-three of the seventy-eight years, there was no cub or bear present at all. This means that in the remaining fifty-five years, there were seventy-six cubs—or about 1.4 per year. The average duration of the cub markets was 2.3 months.

So what does this mean? First of all, market declines of 5 to 20 percent are very common and should therefore be expected. In fact, we should expect one or more every three out of four years. This is normal market activity. (But remember, bull markets still occur 80 percent of the time.) Therefore, market hiccups are not only normal, but even desired. Yes, desired. Why? Let's take a look.

Further analysis of our data revealed that in the thirty days following a cub or bear market, the S&P 500 gained an average of 4.65 percent. On eight of the eighty-nine occasions, double-digit increases occurred in the first month.

It is clear that if investors can understand the normal fluctuations of securities markets, they will be less likely to make the BIG MISTAKE—that is, selling out to avoid a loss. While it may sound trite, the only sure way to lose money in the market, absent proper super-diversification, is to sell out. Knowing how quickly the markets have historically bounced back after these common adjustments, whether bear or cub, gives investors the information they need to stay the course and take advantage of the tremendous growth that can be attained with the proper amount of patience.

Here is the dangerous situation you must avoid: If you have just been burned by the markets and decide to get out so you can sleep at night, what are the chances that you will get right back in given your emotional state? Will you get back in within thirty days . . . ninety days . . . a year? It is likely you will wait at least some period of time beyond thirty days to regain your confidence. However, if you have the proper understanding of the market cycles, whether cub, bear, or bull, you will be in a position to take advantage of market forces and get plenty of restful slumber. Heck, you might even consider hibernating.

PARADIGM SHIFT: THE MRP FUTURE VALUE

If it is true that capital market returns are truly available for all, then it is imperative that we, as investors, change our way of thinking about our portfolios—including the size of our holdings.

For example, if a tax-deferred portfolio (such as an IRA) is worth $1 million today and receives a return of 10 percent, its value will be $10,834,705 in twenty-five years. Do you not then own a $10.8 million asset and not a $1 million asset if this growth is there for the taking? We have labeled this concept the MRP Future Value.

What is the future value of your current portfolio? Do you have any relative certainty of its ultimate growth?

You must concern yourself with the best possible way to create and protect the market return (the $10.8 million) that is rightfully yours as fortunate participants in the great capitalist system we have inherited. Furthermore, as good stewards, are we not all obligated to protect the full future value of our assets for ourselves, our children, and our grandchildren?

You may ask, "Why do I want market return?" Some investors are concerned about the risk involved in the stock market and shy away from stocks. Others are not satisfied with receiving only market return, thinking they can beat the market. Therefore we will answer this question for both parties.

FEAR ITSELF

First of all, we'll speak to the group that is, to put it bluntly, afraid of stocks.

The long-term goal of investors should be to protect their purchasing power. In overcoming the insidious effects of inflation, stocks are by far the most effective and efficient tools to use. Figure 5.2 below shows the annual compound rate of return for some general asset classes over the last seventy-nine years:[2]

Figure 5.2

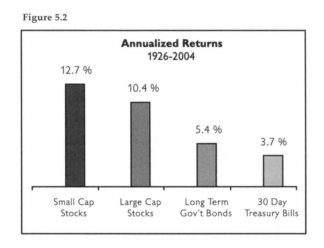

The graph shows the average annualized return of bonds to be approximately half that of stocks. The owners of stocks have clearly had the advantage.

When inflation is taken into consideration, the gap widens even further. This is known as the real rate of return. With inflation averaging approximately 3 percent during this time frame, the return multiple for stocks changes from twice as much to three or four times as much as bonds. (Figure 5.3)[3]

Figure 5.3

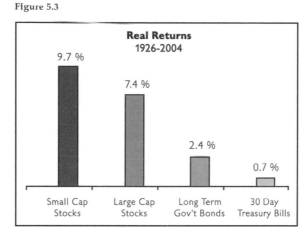

When we consider the higher marginal tax rates of bond interest (potentially 35 percent) versus the capital gains and dividend treatment available in equities (15 percent or even 5 percent at lower income levels), we have the makings of a huge gap, as seen in Figure 5.4[4]. These results show a definite advantage to holding stocks versus bonds when the effects of inflation and taxes are brought to bear on a long-term portfolio. (Income tax rates have fluctuated over the last eighty years. We used 2004 rates to illustrate the point.)

Figure 5.4

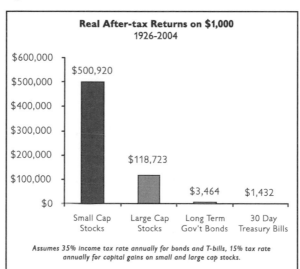

Even after seeing these numbers, many will say, "Stocks are still too risky for me." This sentiment is widely held—especially among investors nearing retirement age. But it's simply not valid.

This fear of stocks is born out of two misperceptions:

1. **Investors do not understand the meaning of long term.**

2. **Investors do not really know what true portfolio risk is.**

WHAT IS LONG TERM?

Almost all portfolios (with just a few exceptions) are long term in nature. Exceptions would include portfolios designed to save for a down payment on a house, to pay off short-term business debt or those designed for putting money aside for a college education. In all of these cases, the money has an end point when it will all be used for a specific expenditure in a given time frame. Even at that, the college education fund can and should be invested for capital appreciation—especially early in a child's life.

If a nest egg is needed for any type of income generation—it should be considered a long-term investment. With retirees living longer, this income may be needed for thirty or forty years after retirement. The temptation for many people nearing retirement is to go to a large bond or fixed-income position to protect the investment and get yield. Yet, as we have seen, the total return for stocks versus bonds is not even close—especially when inflation and taxes are considered. Even money that is set aside for an inheritance should be positioned to grow and benefit the heirs for whom it is intended.

Whether you are in preretirement, retired, or at a stage in your life when you want to leave a legacy for loved ones or a cause in which you deeply believe, all portfolios should be managed in such a way as to achieve real growth. That means planning for the long term and using equities.

WHAT IS INFLATION?

"Inflation is when you pay fifteen dollars for the ten-dollar haircut you used to get for five dollars when you had hair." —Sam Ewing

Here's a quick question: would you rather buy a one-year Treasury bond that paid 11.2 percent in 1980 or one that yielded 5.9 percent in 2000? The answer seems obvious—the higher yield is preferable. But believe it or not, the better investment was the 2000 Treasury bond, even though the yield was 47 percent less than in 1980. The difference, of course, is the rate of inflation that investors were experiencing during each time period. Prices rose over 12 percent in 1980, while they climbed only 3.4 percent in 2000.[5]

WHAT IS PORTFOLIO RISK?

With long-term thinking established, we turn our attention to the second part of the misperception concerning a fear of stocks—the real meaning of portfolio risk. The first definition of risk in most dictionaries is: the possibility of suffering harm or loss. This is the definition that comes to mind for most investors who are afraid of losing their money—or their principal. However, in a proper investing context, we are not content to protect only our principal—but rather our purchasing power—which encompasses our principal and its future growth and income (i.e., total return).

As we dig deeper into the list of dictionary meanings for risk we discover this additional definition: the variability of returns of an investment. The word variability is a beautiful word to investors who are seeking market return. Variability means the quality, state, or degree of being variable or changeable.

Most people generally dislike change and often assign a negative connotation to it. However, when something is changeable, the potential to become better also exists. Change does not inherently connote a negative. When we invest we want changes. Why? Because the vast majority of the time, change in a securities market is a positive experience—not negative (see again Figure 5.1)! Therefore, if we can embrace the power of change and realize through a study of ample data that free markets must grow over time—then we can have confidence that taking on all the risk the market has to offer means we have a greater opportunity for positive change. Ironically and not intuitively, herein lies the basis for genuine portfolio protection.

WARS AND RUMORS

Whenever we are at war, the prevailing question investors ask is, "What effect will a war have on my portfolio?" While the question may be largely unanswerable, it is somewhat helpful to look at the effects that armed conflicts have had through the years. The chart below shows the annualized returns of two major US market indices[6] the year a conflict actually occurred as well as in the following three-year period:

Conflict	Time Period	S&P 500	Small US Co.
World War II	1941	-11.58	-10.03
	1942-1944	21.96	45.61
Korea	1950	31.74	38.25
	1951-1953	13.27	6.41
Cuban Missile Crisis	1962	-8.73	-17.43
	1963-1965	17.17	22.89
Vietnam	1964	16.51	17.14
	1965-1967	7.84	30.42
Desert Storm	1991	30.55	48.83
	1992-1994	6.26	11.56
Iraqi Freedom	2003	28.69	58.46

First of all, we can make some general observations. The effects in the year the conflicts began have varied. The stock markets were largely negative in the year World War II began and during the Cuban Missile Crisis, but were up considerably the years each of the other four conflicts began. However, it is difficult to draw much of a conclusion from this information given the fact that both WWII and the Cuban incident took place late in their respective calendar years. Second, and perhaps most significant, the average three-year period returns following the year the conflicts started were all positive, with most up significantly.

These data suggest a couple of things. One, it could be argued that the effects of war on the economy were either already factored into the markets or became factored in early in the conflict. And two, while the news from each conflict was at times very bad, it was still only one factor in the world's most powerful economy, which is affected by numerous other economic factors each day.

The conflict with Iraq was spawned out of the war on terrorism, which brought with it a new realization of global insecurity. In this regard, it is similar to the Cuban Missile Crisis, which was technically not an armed conflict. However, it too was an alarm clock that awoke the American consciousness. While the Cold War was at full throttle in 1962, it was also an ocean away. The Cuban crisis brought the threat of ending the American way of life within ninety miles of our shore—a wakeup call, to say the least. Even though the crisis was averted, the threat remained firmly embedded in the psyche of our society from that point on. Yet capital markets rose over the next three-year period (and beyond).

There is no reason to believe that a free economy and free markets will do anything other than survive and ultimately thrive after any future conflicts—unless we are unwilling to protect freedom (and thus free markets) when threatened. The irony is that the only way economic survival and prosperity is maintained in both times of war and times of peace is to protect the freedom we hold so dear. This has always enabled us to recover.

THE RESILIENCY OF THE STOCK MARKETS

How can we gain confidence that change will usually be a positive experience? The key here is to understand the positive effects that time has on money invested in free markets. For example, if you were to look closely at the S&P 500 Index over the last seventy-nine years you could easily see how time in the market mitigates negative downturns and has proven positive the overwhelming majority of the time. Meaning, over the long haul, it continues an upward trend.

Figure 5.5

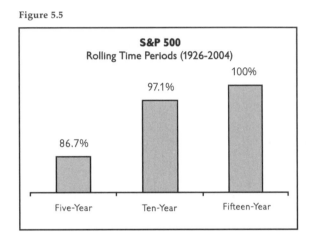

S&P 500
Rolling Time Periods (1926-2004)

As seen in Figure 5.5[7], when we look at any five-year rolling time frame, positive returns occur nearly 90 percent of the time. When ten-year or fifteen-year rolling time frames are observed, positive returns occur 97 percent to 100 percent of the time! Furthermore, since the Great Depression (1929 to 1932), the S&P 500 Index has never had a four-year period of time when it lost ground each year. The most recent three-year losing streak was from 2000 through 2002. However, just like clockwork, 2003 came roaring back, growing a healthy 28.7 percent.

With this incredible track record in mind, consider all of the events that have occurred since the 1920s: World War II, the Korean War, Sputnik, the Cuban Missile Crisis, the assassination of President Kennedy, the Vietnam War, President Nixon's resignation, hyperinflation, Iran hostages, oil embargoes, Black Monday, the Persian Gulf War, President Clinton's impeachment, the terrorist attacks of 9/11, and the Iraq war. Furthermore, three of these events in particular had a sudden and shocking impact on the psyche of the American people and on the securities markets. The surprise attack on Pearl Harbor was instigated by a rogue nation in search of global dominance. The Kennedy assassination was carried out by a supposed lone gunman of counter-political persuasion. The 9/11 attacks in New York and Washington were perpetrated by terrorist groups not affiliated with any single sovereign government.

While all of these events were different, all threatened the very fabric of our society; and in the case of Pearl Harbor, even the existence of our society. These events had a negative impact on the stock markets. The chart below shows the number of days it took the Dow Jones Industrial Average to recover to pretragedy levels.

Tragedy	Date	DJIA Closing	Days to Recover
Pearl Harbor	December 7, 1941	112.52	334
Kennedy Assassinated	November 22, 1963	711.49	4
9/11	September 11, 2001	8920.70	59

We can see that the recovery from these horrific events was relatively short as the billions of daily economic factors took control and overcame the negative effects. Capital markets are resilient even in the very worst of circumstances.

2003: ANOTHER CASE IN POINT

When we consider the results of the equities markets in a year like 2003, how could anyone have ever predicted what would transpire? Consider the following: the SARS epidemic from Asia, the start of the Iraq war, the plunging US dollar, the mutual funds scandal, continued malfeasance in major corporations, and reports of an overall weak economy with slow job growth. Yet in the midst of all of this, a stock investor would have had to be completely unlucky to earn less than 25 percent. The large cap US stocks had their best year in the last five, large international stocks had their best in the last seventeen, and microcap stocks had their best year in thirty-six years.[8]

The Dow Jones Industrial Average hit its low on March 11 at 7,524 and then proceeded to climb almost 3,000 points by the end of the year.

Investors were naturally nervous early in the year due to all the bad news. Many stayed on the sidelines watching as the bad news continued and the stock market climbed. The lesson: Get in and stay in. Bad news and events will have an effect on the markets, but they will recover.

No other nation or economic system has ever existed like the one we are blessed to be a part of now. In light of this phenomenon we call capitalism, optimism is the only logical reality. Fear of loss should be replaced by hope of change. Hence, investors can see investment fluctuations in a whole new light. You should no longer mistake variability for loss, and you should desire to have market return through positive market change. Given this paradigm, we can now argue that stocks are actually safer than bonds when our objective is to protect our long-term purchasing power.

Does this mean we should never own bonds in our portfolios? No. We'll talk more about their proper role soon.

THREE'S A CHARM

When investors are in the midst of a bad market cycle, they tend to assume that the next year will be the same as the last. This is a dangerous assumption to make. History punishes return speculators time and again for being poor market extrapolators.

Consider this: The most difficult stock market periods in the last century have been the Great Depression (1929–1932), pre-WWII (1939–1941), post-Vietnam (1973–1974) and the post-tech-bubble bear market period (2000–2002). However, we see that both bad and good markets come in spurts of three years or less, with only a few exceptions. One exception is the 1929–1932 period of four bad years. Another is the more recent 1995–1999 bull market, which lasted five years. Other than these, it is difficult to find an asset class with longer periods of distinct ups or downs.

The other interesting piece of data in relation to the short-term behavior of markets is the fact that when the trends shift in the other direction, they do so with whiplash speed. For example, during the 1939–1941 decline, the S&P 500 lost an average of 7.4 percent per year. In 1942–1944, it subsequently gained an annual average of 22 percent. In 1973–1974, it lost an average 20.8

percent each year but gained an average 30.4 percent the next two years (1975–1976). For this same time period, the turnaround was even more dramatic for small cap stocks: a 35.2 percent loss and 62.0 percent gain, respectively. For international companies, the index dropped an average 18.2 percent each year, only to rebound with an average gain of 19.2 percent during 1975–1976.[9] The real winners in the long-term investment arena will be those who stay the course by diversifying their equities among multiple asset classes and accepting the returns that will inevitably come. To borrow from Abraham Lincoln: "Let no feeling of discouragement prey upon you, and in the end you are sure to succeed."

WHAT ARE THE ODDS?

As we mentioned earlier concerning the question, "Why do I want market return?" there are those who ask this question with the idea in mind that they can beat the market. Therefore, they are not interested in settling for anything less. But over any significant period of time it is not only unlikely, it is highly improbable that anyone can consistently beat market return.

In the first half of the book we spent considerable time discussing active management techniques and their failings. We explained how timing and picking lead to a belief that an investor can chase returns successfully. The reality is that the overwhelming majority of active managers actually end up providing less return than the market would freely give. In order to drive this point home once and for all, we will engage in a little exercise in probability.

If market return is truly there for the taking, then the ratio of our chance of getting market return would have to be 1:1. Stated differently, we would have a 100 percent (one out of one) chance of getting market return. Exactly how market return is achieved will be discussed in the next chapter. (But for now, we will work under the 1:1 assumption.)

We would submit that proper portfolio diversification demands that we invest in at least four different stock asset classes, for example, large US blend companies, large US value, small US value, and large international. (Note that asset classes are not the same as sectors such as technology, utilities, or biomedical.) Most likely, we would use somewhere between six and fifteen asset classes, including bonds. However, for our discussion, four will easily make the point.

By researching all of the various mutual fund managers in the universe, we find, as shown in Figure 5.6, how many active managers in each category beat their market benchmark (or index) in 2004.[10]

Figure 5.6

Asset Class	Funds	Beat Index	%
Large US Blend	321	96	30
Large US Value	297	78	26
Small US Value	156	61	39
Large International	251	74	29

As you can see from the chart, a mere 30 percent of the active large US blend company managers beat their benchmarks in the one-year period. The ratio or chance of this being accomplished therefore is less than one out of three. The other three asset classes achieved percentages of 26 percent, 39 percent and 29 percent, respectively, in the one-year period. The next question we would ask is: "What are the chances that we could pick active managers who beat their benchmark indices in each of the four asset class categories for the one-year period?" The calculation is as follows:

$$.30 \times .26 \times .39 \times .29 = 0.882\%$$
or 1:113

What does this mean? It means that you have a 1 in 113 chance of finding money managers that can beat the market in each of the four asset classes. This compares with a 1 in 1 chance of getting market return in all four. So which is more attractive? Keep in mind we are looking at the probability of achieving this in just one year.

What about the probability of stringing the last five or ten or thirty years together to build a portfolio that consistently beats the market each year? Here are the numbers in the same asset class order as in Figure 5.6.

5 Years: .040 x .029 x .051 x .069 = 0.0004082% or 1 in 244,975
10 and 30 years = LOTTERY-LIKE ODDS

The numbers become unrealistic.

As we saw in chapter 3, chasing returns is a natural tendency among investors who seek to beat the market using active trading techniques. The data here show it is highly unlikely that such speculative habits would mesh with the buy-and-hold stance needed to patiently wait out a manager's poor years. Most investors would jump ship after one, two, or certainly three bad years.

WHAT ABOUT RISK-ADJUSTED RETURNS?

All too often investors focus on return and forget the importance risk plays in a portfolio. While it is true that taking more risk generally provides a higher return in the long-term, we would suggest that you should take only the amount of risk necessary to achieve market return. (Racecar driver Johnny Rutherford once said, "The important thing is to win at the slowest speed possible.")[11] For example, if an active fund manager is beating his benchmark index, but taking 40 percent more risk than the market risk to do so, the risk-adjusted return is likely not worth it.

Figure 5.7 shows the same results we discussed before when adjusted for market risk.[12] In other words, the same comparisons including only those managers who took the same risk as the S&P 500 Index, or less, and still beat their benchmark in 2004.

Figure 5.7

Asset Class	Funds	B*<=1	%
Large US Blend	321	56	17
Large US Value	297	45	15
Small US Value	156	46	30
Large International	251	44	18

*B = Beta, a measurement of volatility or risk. Generally, the market risk is
presumed to have a beta of 1.0. The higher the beta, the higher the risk.

As you can see from the chart, 17 percent of the active large US blend managers beat their benchmark in the one-year period with equal risk as the S&P 500 Index, or less. The ratio or chance of this being accomplished therefore is approximately one out of six.

The other three asset classes achieved ratios of 15 percent, 30 percent, and 18 percent respectively, in the one-year period. The chances that you could pick active managers that beat their benchmark indices maintaining market risk or less in all four asset classes for the one-year period is as follows:

.17 x .15 x .30 x .18 = 0.137%
or 1 out of 730

Clearly, the numbers are stacked against active management even further when these risk-adjusted data are considered. This shows that the chance of achieving a diversified, lower-risk, actively managed portfolio that beats the market even for one year is highly improbable.

The concepts we have just discussed are a testament to why we almost never see actual clients with actual portfolios that consistently beat the market. We only see individual fund track records for a limited time after the fact. Since no investor owns only one fund (we hope), it is the portfolio return that really matters.

WHAT IS MARKET RETURN?

Investors should be beneficiaries of both the protection and growth that the markets freely give. To show these two very important aspects, we now introduce, in more detail, the concept of a Market Return Portfolio™ (MRP).

One market time frame in particular gives us a wonderful laboratory in which to examine the benefits of getting market return. The period from March 2000 through December 2004 was an excellent testing ground for such a protection and growth study. We saw the worst bear market since the Great Depression followed by a dramatic turnaround into positive territory. Many market timers and stock pickers tout such periods of volatility as the perfect environment for them to apply their craft. Let's then compare the results in this interesting time frame.

Figure 5.8 shows the results of stock indices during the bear market of March 2000 to November 2002. We'll call it the Bear Chart.

Figure 5.8

Bear Period Return
March 1, 2000 to October 31, 2002

Indices	Total Return
Dow Jones Industrials	-13.09%
S&P 500 Index	-32.71%
NASDAQ	-71.48%
Russell 2000	-32.48%
EAFE (International)	-41.57%
Market Return Portfolio Models	
Equity (100% Equity)	-8.95%
Aggressive (80% Equity)	-3.18%
Balanced (60% Equity)	2.67%

For the sake of comparison, we also tracked three Market Return Portfolio models.[13] As you can see, the MRP strategy was very effective at buffering the ill effects that this deep bear market created. We coined a term for this type of protection. We call it the *giant portfolio stop-loss effect.* We believe this is the result of the super-diversification found in the asset class funds used in MRPs (details are forthcoming in chapter 6). Because the Aggressive and Balanced MRP models have some fixed income contained in them, the best apples-to-apples comparison is found when we look at the Equity MRP strategy, which is composed of 100 percent stock funds. As we can see, it lost only 8.95 percent during this thirty-two-month period as the major stock indices plummeted in comparison. Imagine owning nothing but stocks during this deep bear market—and still losing only about 3.4 percent per year.

We next review the time period from November 2002 through December 2004. We call this our Bull Chart (Figure 5.9[14]).

Figure 5.9

Bull Period Return
November 1, 2002 to December 31, 2004

Indices	Total Return
Dow Jones Industrials	34.85%
S&P 500 Index	42.23%
NASDAQ	63.64%
Russell 2000	79.28%
EAFE (International)	68.38%
Market Return Portfolio Models	
Equity (100% Equity)	84.30%
Aggressive (80% Equity)	65.31%
Balanced (60% Equity)	48.06%

This period shows a dramatic reversal from the previous thirty-two months. All the stock indices showed a marked improvement during these twenty-six months. Note that the NASDAQ index came back over 60 percent during this time period. However, the 71.5 percent it lost in the bear market meant that it had to gain over 200 percent in order to reach its original level before the bear market began. This shows the exponential damage that can occur in difficult markets. This is why investors should be very aware of the protection element in their portfolio allocations, which is provided by super-diversification.

While we are generally looking to match market returns, the results of this chart show that the MRP strategies[15] outpaced the major index averages. We want to emphasize that this higher performance occurred in a short sample time frame. We will examine longer periods of time soon.

Upon further consideration, we attributed this MRP outperformance to the super-diversification effect of the portfolios as the market quickly grew out of the bear market. The super-diversification effect is simply the concept that asset classes, once combined, have less risk and thus less volatility as the risk is spread. Figure 3.1, discussed earlier, shows this very clearly.

Figure 5.10[16] shows the two time periods we have analyzed in combination: March 2000 through December 2004.

Figure 5.10

The Composite Chart
March 1, 2000 to December 31, 2004

Indices	Total Return
Dow Jones Industrials	17.19%
S&P 500 Index	-4.29%
NASDAQ	-53.32%
Russell 2000	20.42%
EAFE (International)	-1.49%
Market Return Portfolio Models	
Equity (100% Equity)	67.81%
Aggressive (80% Equity)	60.08%
Balanced (60% Equity)	51.99%

Several interesting observations can be made. First apparent is the fact that three of the indices remained in negative territory even though the bull market had been in effect for twenty-six months. The deep losses experienced during the bear period have not yet been overcome. In contrast, the MRP models[17] have made their way well into positive territory. Once again, the protection element provided by the wide and deep diversification of the MRPs during the bear period allowed them to avoid playing catch-up to the same degree as the indices.

Additionally, the extended market also enhanced the performance in this time period. The extended market is the portion of the market not included in the indices. Many of these excluded companies are included in the institutional asset class funds used in the MRP.

Now if the indices fared in this manner, how did the actual mutual fund managers perform in this same composite time frame (March 2000 through December 2004)?

Average Period Return for Actively Managed US Stock Mutual Funds: 14.37 percent[18]

This is only about one-fifth of the return of the Equity MRP model (67.81 percent), which represents market return that is there for the taking. Remember, this average return for active managers is also subject to survivorship bias, which eliminates thousands of the underperforming funds that were merged or closed. Without the effect of survivorship bias, this percentage would have been even lower.

After seeing the data concerning these fifty-eight months, it begs the question, "What about longer time periods?" Does the MRP strategy work well over the long haul? In this regard, Figure 5.11[19] gives the results of the twenty-year period from 1985 through 2004.

Figure 5.11

20-Year Annualized Return January 1, 1985 to December 31, 2004	
Indices	**Total Return**
Dow Jones Industrials	14.58%
S&P 500 Index	13.23%
NASDAQ	11.09%
Russell 2000	11.54%
EAFE (International)	11.42%
Market Return Portfolio Models	
Equity (100% Equity)	16.11%
Aggressive (80% Equity)	14.55%
Balanced (60% Equity)	12.93%

As you can see, the overall objective of receiving market return holds true for this longer time period as well. This chart shows a more normalized result for the MRP strategy[20] as it provides performance roughly equal (although somewhat higher on average in this sample) to the market on a consistent basis. Consistency—the 1:1 probability of getting a dependable representation of market performance—is the key element in the MRP methodology. Without this 1:1 component, investors are left twisting in the wind as they try to beat the lottery-like odds that active management offers. Lack of consistency is the Achilles heel of active management portfolio strategies.

PRAY FOR A BAD YEAR (?)

Naturally, we are not serious about this. But certainly MRP investors have little to fear from bad years if they remain disciplined and steadfast in their strategy.

By taking a close look at results of the Market Return Portfolio Equity model[21] over a 32-year time frame, we see that each time a "bad year" or two occurred (on three occasions) the results in the following years were phenomenal. In fact, the average return was 43.3 percent in the three post-bad-market years of 1975, 1991, and 2003.

Year	MRP Equity	Year	MRP Equity
1973	**-19.11**	1989	26.25
1974	**-23.72**	**1990**	**-12.59**
1975	49.88	1991	34.11
1976	31.93	1992	11.09
1977	17.49	1993	27.13
1978	23.25	1994	3.16
1979	19.25	1995	22.63
1980	26.87	1996	17.78
1981	6.87	1997	14.17
1982	18.29	1998	6.13
1983	33.11	1999	19.72
1984	7.74	2000	0.10
1985	37.66	2001	1.42
1986	28.65	**2002**	**-9.77**
1987	11.51	2003	46.03
1988	25.87	2004	22.67

The success of the upturn also continued for several years following each of these bad markets. After a combined drop of 42.83 percent in 1973-74, the next 15 years saw growth of 364.62 percent with no negative years and an average increase of 24.31 percent per year. After a drop of 12.59 percent in 1990, the win streak picked up again with eleven straight years of positive numbers, growing a combined 157.44 percent or 14.31 percent per year on average. The most recent year, 2002, which saw a total drop of 9.77 percent was followed by an upturn of 68.7 percent in 2003-04.

These historical data give us confidence that a super-diversified MRP strategy buffers the ill effects of bad years and allows us to prosper in the inevitable and frequent good market periods. MRP participants should simply not fear a bad year in the stock markets.

So now should we go so far as to pray for a bad year? Of course not. But perhaps when we see it happen, we can say a prayer of thanksgiving that we live in a free-market society that can ultimately allow us to be successful long-term investors.

A MULTI-TIME FRAME COMPARISON

For further validation of a market return strategy, Figure 5.12 shows the ten-year rolling returns for a simulated MRP Equity model,[22] which is composed of stocks only. The diagonal shaded boxes represent the average annualized return for each rolling ten-year period. Note that the annual average returns for all periods are in double digits with the exception of one (9.7 percent from 1993 through 2002). Imagine making an average annual return of 11.2 percent during the 1994 to 2003 time frame—which included that brutal bear market—and being invested 100 percent in stocks!

We believe these data, along with that previously noted, should give investors sufficient confidence that market return truly is there for the taking on a consistent basis with relatively low volatility. This is true, even with full exposure to the stock markets in a 100 percent stock portfolio.

Figure 5.12

	1/73																														
1/73	-19.1	1/74																													
1/74	-21.5	-23.7	1/75																												
1/75	-2.6	6.9	49.9	1/76																											
1/76	5.1	14.7	40.6	31.9	1/77																										
1/77	7.5	15.4	32.4	24.5	17.5	1/78																									
1/78	9.9	16.9	30.1	24.1	20.3	23.2	1/79																								
1/79	11.3	17.3	27.9	22.9	20.1	21.4	19.5	1/80																							
1/80	13.1	18.7	27.7	23.7	21.7	23.2	23.1	26.9	1/81																						
1/81	12.4	17.1	24.5	20.7	18.6	18.9	17.5	16.4	6.9	1/82																					
1/82	13.0	17.2	23.7	20.4	18.5	18.8	17.7	17.1	12.4	18.3	1/83																				
1/83	14.7	18.7	24.7	21.9	20.5	21.0	20.6	20.9	18.9	25.5	33.1	1/84																			
1/84	14.1	17.7	22.9	20.2	18.8	19.0	18.4	18.1	16.0	19.3	19.8	7.7	1/85																		
1/85	15.7	19.2	24.2	21.9	20.8	21.2	20.9	21.2	20.1	23.6	25.4	21.8	37.7	1/86																	
1/86	16.6	19.9	24.6	22.5	21.6	22.0	21.9	22.2	21.5	24.6	26.2	24.0	33.1	28.6	1/87																
1/87	16.3	19.3	23.5	21.5	20.6	20.9	20.7	20.8	20.0	22.3	23.1	20.8	25.5	19.8	11.5	1/88															
1/88	16.8	19.7	23.7	21.9	21.0	21.4	21.2	21.4	20.7	22.8	23.6	21.8	25.6	21.8	18.5	25.9	1/89														
1/89	17.4	20.1	23.8	22.2	21.4	21.8	21.6	21.9	21.3	23.2	24.0	22.5	25.7	22.9	21.0	26.1	26.3	1/90													
1/90	15.5	17.9	21.2	19.5	18.6	18.7	18.3	18.2	17.4	18.6	18.7	16.7	18.3	14.8	11.6	11.6	5.0	-12.6	1/91												
1/91	16.4	18.8	21.9	20.3	19.6	19.7	19.5	19.5	18.8	20.1	20.3	18.8	20.5	17.8	15.7	16.8	14.0	8.3	34.1	1/92											
1/92	16.1	18.3	21.3	19.8	19.0	19.1	18.9	18.8	18.2	19.2	19.3	17.9	19.2	16.8	15.0	15.7	13.2	9.2	22.1	11.1	1/93										
1/93	16.6	18.8	21.6	20.2	19.5	19.6	19.4	19.4	18.8	19.9	20.0	18.8	20.1	18.1	16.6	17.5	15.9	13.4	23.7	18.8	27.1	1/94									
1/94	16.0	18.0	20.6	19.2	18.5	18.6	18.3	18.2	17.6	18.5	18.5	17.3	18.3	16.3	14.8	15.3	13.7	11.3	18.2	13.4	14.5	3.2	1/95								
1/95	16.2	18.2	20.7	19.4	18.7	18.8	18.6	18.5	18.0	18.8	18.8	17.7	18.7	16.9	15.7	16.2	14.9	13.1	19.1	15.6	17.2	12.5	22.6	1/96							
1/96	16.3	18.2	20.5	19.3	18.7	18.8	18.5	18.5	17.9	18.7	18.8	17.7	18.6	17.0	15.9	16.4	15.3	13.8	18.9	16.0	17.3	14.2	20.2	17.8	1/97						
1/97	16.2	18.0	20.3	19.1	18.5	18.5	18.3	18.2	17.7	18.4	18.4	17.5	18.2	16.8	15.7	16.2	15.1	13.8	18.2	15.7	16.7	14.2	18.1	16.0	14.2	1/98					
1/98	15.8	17.5	19.6	18.5	17.9	17.9	17.6	17.5	17.0	17.7	17.6	16.7	17.3	15.9	14.9	15.2	14.2	12.9	16.6	14.3	14.9	12.5	15.0	12.6	10.1	6.1	1/99				
1/99	16.0	17.6	19.6	18.5	18.0	18.0	17.7	17.7	17.2	17.8	17.8	16.9	17.5	16.2	15.3	15.6	14.7	13.6	17.0	15.0	15.5	13.7	15.9	14.3	13.2	12.7	19.7	1/00			
1/00	15.4	16.9	18.8	17.7	17.2	17.1	16.9	16.8	16.3	16.8	16.7	15.8	16.3	15.0	14.1	14.3	13.4	12.3	15.1	13.2	13.5	11.7	13.1	11.3	9.8	8.3	9.5	0.1	1/01		
1/01	14.8	16.3	18.1	17.0	16.5	16.4	16.2	16.0	15.5	16.0	15.8	15.0	15.4	14.1	13.2	13.3	12.4	11.3	13.8	12.0	12.1	10.3	11.4	9.6	8.0	6.6	6.7	0.8	1.4	1/02	
1/02	13.9	15.3	17.0	15.9	15.3	15.3	14.9	14.7	14.2	14.6	14.4	13.5	13.8	12.6	11.6	11.6	10.7	9.6	11.6	9.8	9.7	7.9	8.5	6.6	4.9	3.1	2.3	-2.9	-4.3	-9.8	1/03
1/03	14.8	16.2	17.9	16.9	16.4	16.3	16.0	15.9	15.4	15.9	15.7	14.9	15.3	14.2	13.4	13.5	12.7	11.8	14.0	12.4	12.6	11.2	12.1	10.9	9.9	9.2	9.9	7.5	10.1	14.8	46.0
	1/73	1/74	1/75	1/76	1/77	1/78	1/79	1/80	1/81	1/82	1/83	1/84	1/85	1/86	1/87	1/88	1/89	1/90	1/91	1/92	1/93	1/94	1/95	1/96	1/97	1/98	1/99	1/00	1/01	1/02	1/03

Source: **Dimensional Fund Advisors**

SUMMARY

Investors must understand that protecting only principal is not enough. If you want to protect your purchasing power for many years to come, use equities.

The prospect of using properly diversified equities is not a scary one, but rather an exciting one when the data are considered. This does not mean that investors can completely avoid periods of down markets. However, the fear should subside when it is understood that this market return and purchasing power protection are available on a consistent basis.

Additionally, the odds are incredibly low that investors can find even a few active managers who can beat the market. The odds are lower still when you consider managers who take risk equal to, or below, the market risk. Given this evidence, why would any investor want to give up market return—especially when it is there for the taking?

Finally, we saw how the giant portfolio stop-loss effect that a market return strategy provides can greatly buffer the negative effects of extreme down markets and thrive with the market (as a whole) in good times. The MRP methodology also works as expected by delivering market return during extended time periods covering several market cycles.

Remember that the probability of getting market return remains at 1:1. In the next chapter we explain how this can be achieved and how to successfully formulate a Market Return Portfolio.

6 Chapter
Building a Market Return Portfolio

Most of us remember learning the Bible story of the wise man who built his house upon solid rock. The rain came down, the streams rose, and the winds blew and beat against that house, but it did not fall because it had a firm foundation. Conversely, the foolish man built his house on sand. When the rain came down, the streams rose, and the winds blew and beat against that house, it fell with a great crash.[1]

In the financial realm, the Market Return Portfolio (MRP) strategy entails building your investment house upon solid ground that can withstand the economic storms that befall it. Why? Because it is built on the bedrock economic system of free capital markets. Building a portfolio using active management is tantamount to building a house upon the sand that will cause it to eventually collapse.

This chapter is designed to give you more detail on just how an MRP strategy can be implemented. This will provide the confidence to move forward with the last investment strategy you will ever need.

THE ROLE OF DIVERSIFICATION

It is one thing to buy stocks when you realize that it is the only place to be in order to beat inflation and attain real growth. It is quite another to do it properly.

We have mentioned diversification throughout our discussion, but before we can explore more details of building a Market Return Portfolio, we must define and discuss what proper diversification actually means.

The key is super-diversification, so called because it transcends or passes beyond the limits of commonly defined diversification.

Diversification is a concept to which nearly all investment advisors give lip service. Unfortunately, few actually ever apply diversification correctly. A classic example of improper diversification was seen in the mid- to late-1990s when the buying of large US stocks—particularly technology stocks—was all the rage. The media and most brokers and advisors were telling investors that the new world economy had changed things. Consequently, they were inclined to be overly weighted in the hot sectors or the flavor of the day. The tech bubble burst in 2000 and quickly brought them back to reality.

THE TULIP BUBBLE

Much has been made of the tech stock bubble bursting in 2000 and the adverse effects this had on improperly diversified portfolios—and rightly so. But as we study behavioral finance we see that this is a phenomenon not peculiar to our period or even our culture. (Once again proving the thesis that human nature has been, and always will be, the same. This is good for MRP investors.)

Another bubble experience took place in the 1590s when events were put in motion in Holland that led to one of the most spectacular get-rich-quick binges in history. A Venetian botany professor brought a collection of unusual bulbs to Holland from Turkey. Over the next decade, the tulip became a popular but expensive item in Dutch gardens. When the flowers were stricken with a nonfatal virus known as mosaic, which caused colored stripes to develop on the tulip petals, speculation in tulip bulbs went wild. Popular taste dictated that the more bizarre the bulb, the greater the cost.

Tulip mania had set in. Bulb prices rose out of control. The more expensive the bulbs became, the more people viewed them as smart investments. Traditional industry in the country was dropped in favor of speculation in tulip bulbs. Everyone imagined that the demand for tulips would last forever and that people all over the world would pay any price for them.

People who claimed prices could not possibly go higher watched their friends make enormous profits. The temptation to join them was irresistible and few Dutchmen sat on the sidelines. In the last years of the tulip craze (which occurred from 1636 to 1637), people bartered their personal belongings, land, jewels, and furniture to obtain the investment vehicle they thought would make them rich.

As happens in all speculative crazes, tulip prices eventually soared so high that some people decided they should sell. Soon others followed until a snowball effect took over. Panic reigned in no time. The government stated officially that there was no reason for tulip bulbs to fall in price—but no one listened. Dealers went bankrupt and most bulbs became practically worthless, selling for no more than the price of an onion.[2]

The comparisons that can be made between this historical event and those experienced in the tech bubble are obvious and painful. How do investors avoid the doom of past mistakes? The answer is in the question itself—they become investors and not speculators.

Diversification is the most critical and misunderstood element of investing. Many believe they have proper diversification because they have multiple individual securities or mutual funds. Headlines similar to "How to Diversify With Only Ten Stocks" can add to the confusion. Here are four problems associated with improper diversification:

1. **Using individual securities.** Very few investors have enough capital to diversify properly by purchasing thousands of individual stocks. (And it does take that many, by the way.) They are lulled into believing that holding thirty or forty stocks protects them from loss.

2. **Blue Angel syndrome.** This occurs when too many securities in the same asset class—either individual stocks or mutual funds—are held within the same portfolio. When the asset class is doing well, the positions all soar in precise formation like the Blue Angels F-18 flight team. However, when the market cycle turns, they may all crash together as well.

3. **Overlap.** Many investors understand that mutual funds help diversify from the first dollar. The mistake occurs when they fail to realize that many fund families have considerable overlap within the family of funds. This means that two differently named funds may hold many of the same securities, which undermines the diversification goal.

4. **Dumping "bad" funds.** This is simply the same as chasing returns. Investors should actually want to see at least one of their asset classes doing poorly at all times. This indicates that they are properly diversified because individual asset classes have dissimilar price movements. These divergent movements are the key to overall portfolio performance. Remember, you should not be concerned about individual fund performance because the asset class cycle will turn positive with time if given the chance.

As we saw in the bull and bear charts in chapter 5, broad and deep asset class diversification mitigates the losses in bad markets. We called this the giant portfolio stop-loss effect. Now, technically there is no such thing as buying a stop-loss on an entire portfolio, as is possible with an individual stock position. But a super-diversification strategy basically provides that same type of safety net. Super-diversification also allows an opportunity to share in the market return when the bull market runs again.

The building blocks, or tools, we suggest using to accomplish super-diversification are known as *institutional asset class funds* (IACFs). They allow investors to diversify properly among all the companies in a particular asset class, starting again with the first dollar.

INSTITUTIONAL ASSET CLASS FUND CHARACTERISTICS

The concept for IACFs was born out of Modern Portfolio Theory (MPT). The theoretical foundation for MPT was published by Harry Markowitz in 1952.[3] Along with two associates, Markowitz won the

Nobel Prize in economics in 1990 for his work on the subject. Other academicians naturally gravitated to this logical process.

Interestingly, multimillion-dollar institutional investors, such as pension plans and scholarship funds, have used both asset class mutual funds and Modern Portfolio Theory for some time because of their fiduciary responsibility to protect the investments placed in their trust. They have used these approaches in an effort to reduce the various risks to which their funds are exposed.

In the early 1990s, enterprising individuals implemented the MPT methods by creating the asset class funds now available for individual investors through independent registered investment advisors. Now these same techniques are available for anyone who is interested in the preservation of capital and its steady, long-term growth.

Institutional asset class mutual funds are designed to deliver the investment results of an entire asset class—such as large US value stocks or small international. These asset class funds are best suited to create efficient portfolios that promote super-diversification.

There are four important characteristics of institutional asset class mutual funds:[4]

1. **Lower costs.** The IACFs are true no-load funds. They have no front- or back-end loads, redemption fees, or 12b-1 marketing expenses. They are also 100 percent liquid at all times.[5]

   All mutual funds have operating expenses. These expenses are expressed as a percentage of assets and include management fees, administrative charges, and custodial fees. The average annual expense ratio for all actively managed retail equity mutual funds was around 1.58 percent in 2004.[6] In comparison, the same expense ratio for an institutional asset class portfolio typically averages around 0.40 percent.[7] These lower costs naturally lead to higher net rates of return when compared with more expensive funds.

2. **Reduced turnover.** The average actively managed mutual fund

routinely has turnover rates near 100 percent.[8] This is because they attempt to add performance by trading often within a fund. This high turnover means that if a fund holds one hundred securities at the beginning of the year, at the end of the year nearly all of them would have been sold and perhaps repurchased.

A high turnover ratio usually means that active management (timing and picking) is taking place. This high turnover is costly because, as discussed in chapter 2, other hidden costs including commissions, trading spreads, and market impact costs have a negative effect. These hidden costs can even amount to more than a fund's total operating expenses if the fund trades frequently or if it invests in a more inefficient market (such as small company or international stocks where trading costs can be even higher).

In addition, highly active investors can cause excess turnover by chasing after performance. They move from fund to fund looking for hot asset classes or managers. This can force fund managers to buy and sell even more often than they might like. These return-chasing investors do not pay their fair share of the transaction costs they create. They buy and sell at net asset value (NAV), freeloading on the backs of long-term investors who remain in the funds.

By contrast, institutional asset class mutual funds have low turnover rates. They use objective portfolio filters[9] to determine holdings. This process usually results in a turnover rate of less than 33 percent per year for equity funds.[10] This keeps costs low, which in turn improves performance.

3. **Tax efficiency.** Mutual funds are required to distribute 95 percent of their taxable income each year (including realized capital gains) to remain tax-exempt. Managers do not want to have their fund performance reduced by paying corporate income taxes. Therefore, they distribute all their income annually.

Taxable distributions can have a negative effect on the rates of return of equity mutual funds—particularly those that are involved in active management. The frequent trading that is utilized in an attempt to add value often results in short-term capital gains in a rising market. This means tax rates are in the 35 percent range potentially versus the 15 percent (5 percent for lower incomes) long-term capital gains rate. Because asset class funds are holding their positions based on structured criteria, even the 33 percent turnover is typically more apt to result in long-term gains taxed at the lower 15 percent rate. This inherent characteristic provides much more tax efficiency.

4. **Consistent portfolio allocation.** Research has indicated that the largest determinant of portfolio performance is asset allocation.[11] In other words, how the portfolio is divided among different asset classes. Efficient asset allocation is accomplished when the mutual funds in your portfolio maintain their allocation integrity. Most active managers change their fund asset class percentages over time. They may change their composition by moving from growth to value or small to large or even stocks to bonds. In addition, they often increase or decrease their cash balances based on cash flow requirements and market situations. These ad hoc allocation adjustments, known as fund drift, create portfolio inefficiencies and can significantly change the composition of a portfolio over time.

By using active managers, an investor will give up control of the asset allocation to the managers of the mutual funds. Since the managers do not know each investor's particular situation, they make allocation decisions based on their own needs—not the client's (misaligned interests). A distinct advantage of IACFs in this regard is that they fully maintain their allocation in their assigned asset class at all times. This means that investors are able to maintain their asset class exposures as specified in their investment policy statement.

Now that we have discussed the building blocks themselves, we will combine the principles we have learned to build an efficient Market Return Portfolio model.

USING THE "PORTFOLIO FILTER" FOR FUND MANAGEMENT

Institutional asset class funds use what we refer to as a portfolio filter when determining which securities should be held in a particular fund. Generally, this methodology is designed to eliminate candidates rather than select candidates as active managers do. (That is why we call active managers stock pickers.) This subtle, yet critical, difference is the foundation of passive asset class investing. It is the key ingredient that eliminates the human element in money management that so often derails the most disciplined of investors. By using objective filtering criteria instead of subjective selection, the consistency of the Market Return Portfolio approach to investing is achieved. The following filter chart is a sample of how a US small cap asset class fund committee might create a portfolio.

Initial Universe	5,120
Reason for not buying at this time:	
Asset class concerns	-503
Foreign stocks, ADRs, REITs	
Pricing concerns	-169
Recent IPO, financial difficulty, in bankruptcy,	
Merger/tender or corporate action	
Trading concerns	-260
Less than 4 market makers, listing requirements,	
Limited operating history	
Miscellaneous	-844
Investment companies, limited partnerships,	
Under consideration, inadequate data, miscellaneous	
Total number dropped	(1,776)
Current buy list	3,344

In this example, we see 5,120 securities that qualify as "small cap" in the asset class universe. Each filter would present a reason not to hold a particular security at this time.

The first one indicates asset class concerns. Perhaps the securities are actually foreign stocks or ADRs (American Depository Receipts) which would not qualify as domestic stocks. Or perhaps there are real estate investment trusts which belong in their own separate REIT asset class fund. You can see that 503 companies were excluded, or filtered, for these reasons.

The next filter category would be pricing concerns. Perhaps they are a recent IPO, in the process of merging with or acquiring other companies, or are having financial difficulty. These are all reasons to wait to include them in the fund. You can see that 169 were dropped out for these reasons.

Trading concerns such as a limited operating history would cause securities to fall out of consideration as well. In this example, 260 were eliminated for this reason.

Other miscellaneous reasons such as inadequate data or the fact that the companies in consideration are actually investment companies or limited partnerships could also eliminate them as candidates at this time. A total of 844 were eliminated for this reason.

In all, 1,776 securities were filtered out, leaving 3,344 companies intact to provide the purest asset class representation, and super-diversification, possible. In addition, the extended market effect that is important in creating an opportunity for additional return is evident in this number. The comparable index to this small cap fund would most likely be the Russell 2000 Index. This asset class fund would contain 1,344 more securities or two-thirds more exposure to the asset class. This exposure would also probably be the smallest of the small companies—or microcap stocks, which often have higher returns themselves.

One other note: In order to avoid exorbitant transaction costs when securities have changes in their market capitalization value, a "buffer zone"—of say 5 percent or so—can be used to eliminate this problem, which occurs as stocks grow from the small cap to midcap range. In other words, if the fund has set the top value for security candidates in this fund at $2 billion, the security's capitalization value would have to reach $2.1 billion before it is sold. This gives it some room for reasonable fluctuations to occur.

CREATING THE MARKET RETURN PORTFOLIO MODEL

Thus far we have considered at length the futility of active management. We have discussed the current investment advisory delivery system and what to ask when seeking an investment advisor. We then studied market return including the role of diversification and the building blocks of the Market Return Portfolio—institutional asset class funds. Now it is finally time to talk about building a portfolio that can allow every investor to triumph and create wealth without worry.

In order to best describe the Market Return Portfolio composition, we will compare it with a diversified index portfolio (DIP) represented by familiar indices.[12] We will view results over a twenty-six-year period from 1979 through 2004 as seen in Figure 6.1.

Figure 6.1

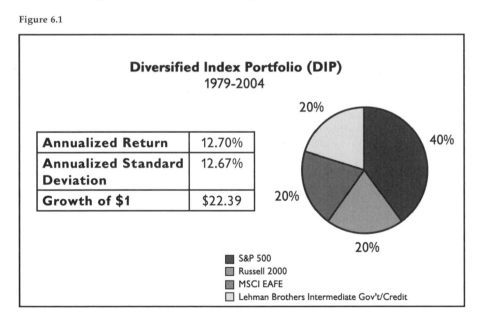

Diversified Index Portfolio (DIP) 1979-2004	
Annualized Return	12.70%
Annualized Standard Deviation	12.67%
Growth of $1	$22.39

■ S&P 500
■ Russell 2000
■ MSCI EAFE
▨ Lehman Brothers Intermediate Gov't/Credit

Knowing what you now know about stock returns versus bonds, having a 100 percent equity portfolio should no longer be a scary proposition. However, most investors will ultimately require some fixed income in their retirement years for cash flow purposes. Therefore, we will use as an example a model that contains an 80:20 stock-to-bond ratio using four common indices of the S&P 500 Index, the Russell 2000 Index, the MSCI EAFE (International) Index and the Shearson-Lehman Government/Corporate Bond Index. This type of allocation is fairly common among investors who are referred to as indexers.

We like the indexing approach from the standpoint that it ignores ineffective active management techniques. However, our objective is to create an 80:20 model that will bring about the purest representation of the market and thus truly be a portfolio that delivers the highest probability of receiving market return.[13] If the MRP approach either increases return or lowers risk, we consider it desirable. If it happens to do both, then we really have hit a grand slam.

Figure 6.2

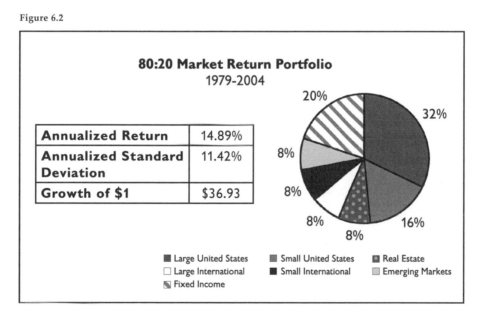

The first observation we can make as we compare Figures 6.1 and 6.2[14] involves the average annualized return. The diversified index portfolio (DIP) returned an average of 12.70 percent per year for the period shown (Figure 6.1). Most investors who have memories of the bear market of 2000 to 2002 would likely be happy to sign a contract for that twenty-six-year performance right now. However, the 80:20 MRP model shows a return of 14.89

percent per year—more than two percentage points higher than the DIP.

Before we look at just what this means to an investor in the way of actual dollars, we must first consider other expenses that come into play.

The average weighted expense ratio for index mutual funds to implement the DIP would likely be around 0.25 percent. We reduced the net annualized performance from 12.70 percent to 12.45 percent to account for this. Additionally, while the 14.89 percent return of the MRP already includes the mutual fund expense ratio, we must also subtract a fee for the independent Registered Investment Advisor (RIA). By subtracting a fee of 0.50 percent, the MRP return is now reduced to 14.39 percent. With this in mind, the difference in return is now reduced to 1.94 percent in favor of the 80:20 MRP strategy.

Now, 1.94 percent is a big number in the investing world. To illustrate just how big, let's see what it translates to in terms of actual dollars. Figure 6.3 shows the effects of this difference on a $100,000 portfolio over twenty-six years.

Figure 6.3

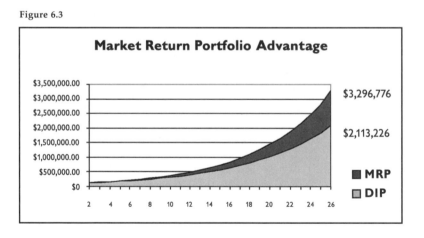

The $100,000 in the 80:20 MRP would have grown, after the fees mentioned were subtracted, to approximately $3.3 million versus about $2.1 million for the DIP. That is a difference of $1.2 million, or 56 percent more dollars. This clearly shows how valuable small percentages can be over time. (And remember, most portfolios should be considered long-term. There are few exceptions.) For fun, we also looked at the same for a $1,000,000 portfolio. What was the difference in twenty-six years? A whopping $11.8 million more in the 80:20 MRP model.

In chapter 2 we spoke of shifting your paradigm concerning the way you should think about your portfolio (ten-plus million versus one million). With market return being there for the taking, the numbers above should make you keenly aware of what you are giving up if you choose not to participate in that which is rightfully yours in a free capital market.

Additionally, the MRP strategy would have delivered this substantially higher return at the same time it exposed the investor to 10.9 percent less risk. (This is measured by the standard deviation or volatility of each portfolio: 11.42 for the 80:20 MRP versus 12.67 for the DIP.)

More return, less risk. Exactly what every investor desires and deserves.

WHY IS THE MRP STRATEGY SUPERIOR TO COMMON INDEX STRATEGIES?

The performance and risk (standard deviation) data we have just examined make a strong case for using institutional asset class funds in a Market Return Portfolio instead of index funds. It should be restated at this point that every investor's primary objective should be to simply mirror, as closely as possible, the return and risk of the market. To this end, the MRP strategy is superior to simple indexing for the following reasons:

1. **Indexes are active management light.** The S&P 500 Index is probably the most widely held investment by individual investors who use index funds. It is continually reconstituted on a monthly basis by a committee that tries to select a group of stocks that are representative of the US economy. This committee selection approach borders on active management (timing and picking). We call it active management light. As a result of this continuous reconstitution, the index may tend to mirror the hot sectors of the day. This reconstitution also unwittingly creates a situation where

index fund managers must buy the new additions to the fund at a higher price. Research shows that the day an announcement is made that a particular company will be added to the index, on average, that company's stock rises 3.2 percent. Subsequently, from the day of the announcement to the actual listing, the price rises an additional 3.8 percent.[15] That is a 7 percent price increase in a very short period of time. This higher price is paid by the fund manager, and thus the fund investors, when the stock is placed in the index. Likewise, the MSCI EAFE Index (International) rise in price is even more pronounced. Estimates have it rising an average of 3.4 percent the day of the announcement and another 4.5 percent in the interim period between announcement and actual listing.[16] With the MRP approach, a hold range—or buffer zone—helps eliminate this situation (see Notes, chapter 6, no. 9 for further explanation). These periodic index changes can also increase the trading costs within the fund.

In another popular index, the Russell 2000, it has been estimated that the index gave up approximately 2 percent in return every year from 1993 through 2004 because of the annual reconstitution.[17] The lack of a buffer zone or security hold range that is characteristic of the MRP approach helps cause this reduction in the return.

In addition, most indexes are not all that good at representing the major asset classes. For example, the Russell 2000 is commonly used to represent the US small cap universe, but this index actually includes some real estate investment trusts (REITs). There's nothing wrong with REITs, it's just that they should not be considered part of the US small cap universe if pure asset class investing is the goal.

2. **The extended market effect.** It is worth repeating that whenever there is additional return, it occurs largely because of the wide and deep super-diversification.

On this point, consider the following: The MRP 80:20 portfolio's institutional asset class funds hold a combined 15,187 individual securities. The DIP represents 3,586 individual securities.[18] This is a difference of 11,601 or over 323 percent more exposure to the equity and fixed-income markets. This exposure to more than 11,000 more companies is also what we referred to as the extended market (as discussed in chapter 5). This is where you can gather a bit more return—return that can add up to a significant amount of dollars over the long term.

3. **The giant portfolio stop-loss effect.** Besides a high probability of better return, the super-diversification which results from using the MRP methodology also creates a giant portfolio stop-loss effect. This is a very important protection element—especially for retirees. This means that in the event of a major corporate collapse, such as with Enron or WorldCom, it is but the very tiniest blip on the radar screen of such a vast number of holdings in the entire Market Return Portfolio. This same protection element has been evident during extreme bear market periods as previously documented. Safety in numbers.

EXCHANGE–TRADED FUNDS

Exchange-traded funds (ETFs) are popular index-type investment vehicles that have made their way to the stage in recent years. Like other index funds, the costs associated with these vehicles are typically low. They were created in a bid to attract smaller investors as well as those who might wish to trade in and out of the market on a daily or even minute-by-minute basis. This is because they are treated like stocks during the trading day versus mutual funds, in which a transaction is conducted based on the day's closing market value. This real-time trading characteristic inherently creates the idea that investors should watch the market closely and buy or sell at just the right moment to take advantage of market moves. This sends an unusual mixed message of "actively traded indexes."

ETFs are also touted as good ways to gain sector exposure in various industries or countries. However, often these types of ETFs can be highly concentrated, with 60 to 75 percent of their holdings in just ten or fewer stocks. This lack of proper diversification creates a real vulnerability to changes in the price of a single security. Additionally, ETFs and other sector specific investment vehicles are subject to "event risk," untimely—sometimes catastrophic—events that adversely affect particular industry sectors or regions of the world. There is no need to expose a portfolio to these types of risks.

Generally, ETFs are comparable to traditional index funds and can be used accordingly. Unfortunately, ETFs will likely remain popular with pickers and timers as they continue to be cleverly marketed. Remember also that ETFs were basically invented by Wall Street because passive investments such as index funds were taking away business.

4. **Index funds promote return chasing and are more prone to panic selling.** Just like with actively managed funds, investors who use index funds or exchange-traded funds (ETFs) tend to want to chase after performance as they see particular indexes or sectors outperform during certain time frames. This is the same old classic investing mistake. They chase after the best-performing index (fund) because they are focusing on the individual pieces of the portfolio rather than the entire portfolio.

Another common problem with index fund investing, which is directly related to chasing returns, is simple panic. Because index funds are easily accessible to even the least sophisticated investor, the fund is full of those who are more prone to knee-jerk reactions to market adjustments. Simply put, they bail out at precisely the wrong times, leaving the more prudent, long-term investors holding the bag. Managers are forced to sell when they know they shouldn't. The resulting transaction costs from these untimely liquidations are passed on to those remaining in the fund.

Those who understand the MRP investing methodology realize that it naturally promotes viewing the portfolio as a whole rather than looking at its component parts, thus discouraging return chasing or imprudent reactions.

5. **Technology and access to IACFs.** Index funds made perfect sense before the early 1990s because they were the only way to avoid active management and its failed investing methods. Although they were only relatively small samples of stocks as compared with the MRP, these index funds gave investors the best opportunity to get the market return they needed. Since then, however, investing has been revolutionized by the advent of computers and the efficient application of Modern Portfolio Theory. As a result, institutional asset class funds (IACFs) are now readily available for use by individual investors through independent advisory firms using the MRP approach.

Investing has become much more of a science than an art. It is worth noting that many of the very same people who introduced and launched indexing as a viable way to invest, progressed to develop asset class mutual funds—the vehicles used in the MRP strategy.

It is time to put away the old, ineffective methods of investing (active management) and outdated tools for achieving market return (indexes). Employing the indexless MRP strategy allows investors to gain all the advantages of passive investing without the baggage associated with index investing. In summary, you can think of it this way: on a scale of 1 to 10, actively managed strategies would be a lowly 1 or 2, index funds and exchange-traded funds would be a 7, and the MRP strategy would be in the 9 to 10 range.

THE ALLOCATION PERCENTAGES

We will now take a closer look at the specific asset classes that make up the 80:20 Market Return Portfolio model.

FIXED INCOME ASSET CLASSES

On the fixed income (or bond) side of the equation, the asset class funds used to construct the MRP model are primarily short term (less than five years) in nature because longer-term bonds generally entail more risk with a diminishing return. This is because bonds have an inverse relationship to interest rates. As interest rates climb, bond values decline and vice versa. Figure 6.4[19] shows this risk-return relationship. The longer the duration of a bond, the greater the risk, and thus the greater the potential decline. By holding shorter-term bonds, you can reduce the erosion of principal in rising-interest-rate periods and maintain a stable portion of the portfolio for monthly income. We included both US and global bond funds in the 80:20 MRP to provide further diversification.

Figure 6.4

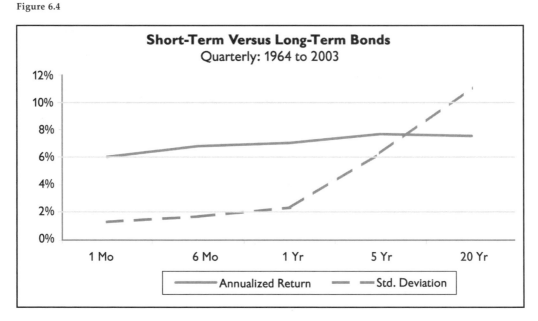

Source: Dimensional Fund Advisors

US EQUITY ASSET CLASSES

The equity (or stock) portion of the allocation has three general areas. As we saw in Figure 6.2, 32 percent of the entire portfolio is made up of large US company funds. These are equally divided between blend and value funds. Small US funds make up 16 percent of the allocation, equally divided again between blend and value.

Finally, a real estate asset class fund, or REIT, contains 8 percent of the allocation. (Depending on the status of real estate ownership outside their portfolio, not all MRP investors will have a REIT fund in their allocation. For example, if investors own rental properties in addition to their homesteads, the REIT allocation may be deleted or reduced. This determination should be made on a case-by-case basis.)

INTERNATIONAL ASSET CLASSES

International market exposure makes up the remaining 24 percent of the portfolio, with the large value, small company and emerging markets each accounting for 8 percent of the allocation.

It is very important to include foreign exposure in a portfolio. Investors often ignore international markets because they regard them as too risky. This is a mistake. Investors also tend to believe that if they own domestic companies that sell products or services overseas, they are investing internationally. Research indicates that stock prices of companies tend to follow the trends of their domiciled country even if a majority of their business comes from foreign markets.[20]

International markets tend to move in different directions than domestic markets. When we say different, this may mean that they are both going up or down, but at a different pace. In the case of foreign markets led by Japan in the mid- to late-1980s, we saw a good example of times when international markets outperformed US markets by a wide margin.[21] Diversification into foreign markets during this and other time frames has preserved capital for many an investor. Typically, a super-diversified Market Return Portfolio would hold 15 percent to 35 percent of its equity exposure in international asset class funds.

VALUE VERSUS GROWTH

It is worth noting that the composition of the equity asset classes has a value emphasis and is largely absent the more popular growth category. Value stocks are categorized as having a high book-value-to-market-value ratio. To many investors, selecting value asset classes over growth asset classes may seem counterintuitive. Most believe that growth would make more sense, especially if that is exactly what they are trying to do—grow their portfolios. However, the research has shown repeatedly that, over the long term, value stocks have indeed outperformed growth stocks (not necessarily in every time frame, but certainly over the long run). This may be because they are inherently riskier, with high book-to-market ratios. Consequently, investors demand a higher return for this added risk. Figure 6.5 shows how dramatic the difference in performance can be over an extended period. [22]

Figure 6.5

Value Versus Growth
1975 to 2004

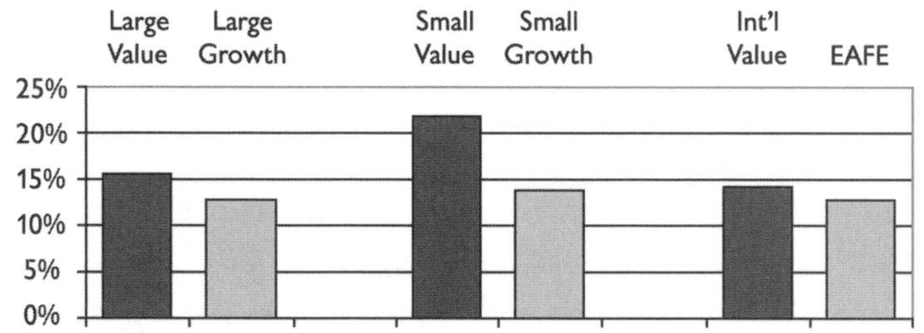

	Large Value	Large Growth		Small Value	Small Growth		Int'l Value	EAFE
Annualized return	15.56%	12.75%		21.79%	13.75%		14.27%	12.76%
Annualized standard deviation	16.00%	16.71%		19.67%	24.26%		16.75%	16.96%
Growth of $1	$76.67	$36.56		$369.99	$47.70		$54.68	$36.72

In the area of large US stocks, we see a 2.81 percent difference in performance, favoring value stocks over this thirty-year period. This would have resulted in more than twice as much growth in actual dollars (Growth of $1). Given this huge difference, along with the fact that the risk taken (standard deviation) was also slightly lower, the value positioning offered a clear advantage. The results are similar in the area of international investing as represented by the EAFE index on the far right of the graph (1.51 percent higher for value stocks).

The most dramatic data are with the small US companies in the middle columns. There was an 8.04 percent performance advantage by the small value asset class, which resulted in approximately seven-and-a-half times more dollars at the end of the period. Additionally, the risk taken would have been about 19 percent less for the value position. More return, less risk—what every investor needs and wants.

We believe these data show that the value positioning is one factor responsible for the return advantage (versus the market) we have seen exhibited by the Market Return Portfolio strategy over the long run. Remember however, this is still just icing on the cake, as your goal should always be to simply get market return with consistency.

MORE ABOUT RISK

On a scale of risk, most investors would rank these general asset classes in the following manner:[23]

Riskiest	Emerging markets
↑↓	Small international
	Small US
	Large international
	Large US
	Real estate investment trusts
	Long-term bonds
	Intermediate bonds
Safest	Short-term bonds

The MRP contains substantial amounts of most of these asset classes that are on all parts of the scale—including the risky end. It is not intuitive to think that by having a portfolio hold substantial amounts of these riskier asset classes it would actually have a lower volatility or standard deviation. But this is witness again to the miracle of super-diversification. Combining asset classes with different risk characteristics or dissimilar price movements actually reduces overall risk in a portfolio.

The risk of the whole is less than the risk of the sum of its parts.

This is one of the most important points to make about super-diversification and the MRP strategy.

THE LOSS-PLUS-TAX TRAP

Having been convinced of the advantages offered by the MRP approach to investing, you may be in a circumstance in which your portfolio is composed of individual securities with a low or very low tax basis. This could translate into a substantial income tax burden if you want to liquidate these individual holdings and implement the MRP strategy immediately. The question you ask yourself is, "Should I sell and take the tax hit now, or try to sell tactically with an eye on spreading the taxes over multiple years?" The temptation is to do the latter and not the former. This is the *loss-plus-tax trap.*

This taxing dilemma demands you make a choice. With this in mind, here are the pros and cons of the situation.

The obvious advantage to gradually selling off individual securities is the avoidance or reduction of capital gains taxes. The disadvantages of this liquidation technique are:

1. **Picking and timing.** You will have to reenter the world of uncertainty after seeing the more certain performance available in the MRP approach. These active management techniques will force you to again make emotional investment choices of when and what to sell.

2. **No super-diversification.** The buffering effect of super-diversification will be lost if individual securities are held. Even with hundreds of securities in your portfolio, the level of downside protection cannot be achieved to the same degree. The standard deviation (risk) in the individual stock portfolio will simply be higher by up to two to three times.

3. **The actual dollar cost.** Because of the inherent failings of picking and timing, you will almost certainly sell the individual securities too early or too late. If a security shrinks in value before you can sell, you will lose 100 percent of the amount you would have paid in taxes on the entire stock sale in the first place. In addition, you would still have to pay long-term capital gains taxes of 10 or 15 percent. These two amounts comprise the loss-plus-tax trap.

Rather than spend time, energy and money following a gradual liquidation strategy, why not pay the tax now and opt for the MRP strategy, which harnesses the power of free capital markets? This gives you a more reliable performance in the form of market return. Super-diversification and a consistent performance can reward you over time with financial security and peace of mind.

The concept outlined to avoid the loss-plus-tax trap is a general principle to consider. There are circumstances when it may be prudent to liquidate an individual stock portfolio in successive calendar years for tax management purposes. Each individual situation is different and extenuating circumstances could arise that require varied solutions based on your tax situation. Therefore, coordination with a professional tax advisor and a written financial plan are of paramount importance.

GOOD NEWS FOR TAX MANAGEMENT

Market Return Portfolio strategies also can be implemented on a tax-managed, tax-deferred, or tax-deductible basis.

For taxable accounts, there are tax-managed institutional asset class funds available that are specifically designed to minimize taxes. These tax-managed funds deliver the same consistent exposure to their asset classes but with a special emphasis on maximizing after-tax returns. These tax-efficient funds seek to offset capital gains and losses. Equity funds generate dividends that traditional management tends to ignore. This is especially true among small cap and value stocks that distribute more income than large cap growth stocks. These tax-managed strategies simultaneously attempt to minimize taxable gains and dividend yield without sacrificing precise asset class exposure and super-diversification.

On the tax-deferred side of the equation, if you have reached the maximum in funding your qualified retirement plan and have a need for additional tax deferral in your financial plan, it may make sense for a portion of your portfolio to be placed in a tax-deferred variable annuity. On the other hand, you may have already been sold a retail variable annuity and you are looking to get out from under the excessive fees that typically exist in them without also incurring income tax and penalties. In both cases, asset class funds are available within institutional variable annuities. In addition, the mortality and expense charges associated with institutional annuities are considerably less than their retail counterparts and they have no surrender penalties.

Lastly, tax-qualified plans that allow tax deductions, such as IRAs, pension plans and the popular 401(k), are also eligible to hold institutional asset class funds. This allows implementation of an MRP strategy for retirement plans as well.

GENERATING INCOME DURING RETIREMENT

A common question asked by retirees is: "How do we get income from our nest egg once we have retired?" A companion concern is that they do not want to be forced to sell a security when its value has dropped in order to have income for their household budget. We discussed earlier the important paradigm-shifting truth that real long-term purchasing power protection comes through owning stocks. Now we must figure out how to provide adequate cash flow without selling low.

The technique is quite simple, actually. It is accomplished through periodic rebalancing. For example, if a retired couple has a 60:40 portfolio mix of stocks to bonds (Figure 6.6), this mix will naturally change over time as market fluctuations occur. After a few months or perhaps a year, the mix may be 65:35 because stocks have outpaced bonds. Conversely, it may be 55:45 if stocks have retreated during the time period. At any rate, the rebalancing will involve resetting the mix to the original 60:40 allocation. To accomplish this, the growing asset class is sold down to its original allocation. That cash is then reallocated into the asset class that shrunk to rebalance the portfolio (Figure 6.7). This rebalancing automatically creates a situation where the investor is selling high (from the asset class that grew) and buying low (into the asset class that fell behind). This automation systematizes the very thing that all investors strive to do—sell high and buy low.

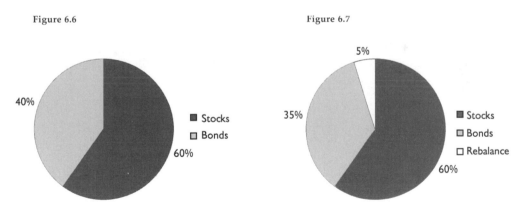

Figure 6.6

Figure 6.7

This rebalancing technique should be used in all portfolios but becomes a special advantage to a retiree. Here's how: First of all, retirees should be taking money for living expenses from the cash/fixed income side of their portfolios. Retirees should hold shorter-term bonds, which have far less volatility. Naturally, when money is taken from the cash/bond side of the portfolio, it reduces the percentage remaining in that asset class. When the rebalancing takes place, equities are sold in order to replenish the cash/bonds position. Consequently, a retiree is only selling the equities that are higher in order to replenish the cash/bond side. If for some reason all stock asset classes are in an extreme bear market, then it may require holding off on the rebalancing for a short time. However, even in the deepest of recessions or bear markets, there are typically one or two stock asset classes that are not way down—perhaps flat. Knowing what we now know about market cycles, as long as retirees have at least four years of living expenses in the cash/bond allocation, chances are very good that they can weather any market storm and have adequate cash flow through a down market—without having to sell equities when they are low.

CAN MRP SAVE SOCIAL SECURITY?

There is no question that the math in the Social Security equation is pretty simple. At the current pace of spending, the system is going to run out of money. It is just a matter of when. The projected date when tax receipts begin to fall short of outlays is around 2017.[24] The system is pay-as-you-go with fewer workers paying for more retirees in a society where life expectancy is now reaching into the eighties. Furthermore, there is no trust fund from which to draw. Increasing tax rates or decreasing benefit payments seem to be the only alternatives in a gridlocked Congress. With this in mind, chances are good that both of these solutions will be applied in the future. Investors under the age of fifty who have used their projected Social Security benefit in their retirement cash flow calculations may want to rethink this approach. In fact, they may want to disregard their Social Security benefits completely just to be safe.

For years now, politicians have floated ideas of just how to save the system. An alternative of allowing personal accounts directed by employees is one example that has received a fair amount of support in the past.

That is, until the bear market time frame of 2000 to 2002. The enthusiasm quickly waned as opponents used risk-of-principal-loss scare tactics.

However, as the debate was reopened with a Bush second term, perhaps a slightly different paradigm should be considered. When market return is there for the taking, can't our leaders see the logic of using free markets to pay for Social Security? Would there be anything wiser than using the power of capitalism to provide a social benefit for all? How can we ignore such an opportunity? After all, the South American nation of Chile figured this out some time ago with a privatized system in which over 90 percent of its workers participate. Nine other industrialized countries, including Great Britain, have also implemented at least partially privatized systems. Surely the greatest nation in the world, with the greatest economic system ever created, can follow suit.

Time will tell whether or not our lawmakers ultimately decide to harness market forces to benefit our citizens. Meanwhile, we had all better be prepared to take ultimate responsibility for our own financial futures. Fortunately, MRP is the tool that can aid all investors as they take action to prepare for their retirement destiny outside the government retirement system.

So, can MRP and free capital markets save Social Security? Yes, if lawmakers let them, we are confident they can. However, the likelihood of that happening in the most efficient manner is very small. The responsible solution is to become an MRP investor!

A FEW MORE THOUGHTS ON THE MARKET RETURN PORTFOLIO

In addition to index funds, we considered comparing the Market Return Portfolio strategy with a portfolio of active managers. The problem is, which ones? With the odds so stacked against finding enough active managers who can beat the market, how can we possibly make the comparison? If we went back and used the best active manager performers over this time frame, we still would be faced with the problems of survivorship and hindsight bias. But no one could have chosen those managers before they performed well (against the astronomical probabilities we spoke of in chapter 5). Even if we assume that we could beat those ridiculous odds, would investors be patient enough with the randomly bad years of managers to stay around for their randomly good years? Human nature tells us this would be extremely difficult. Especially when we consider that the average investment holding period is only about three years.[25]

With MRP, on the other hand, we did not data mine and find the best performers because the institutional asset class funds simply represent the market in the purest form. The results are what they are. There is no picking of these funds based on their past performances. The strategy affords basically one alternative—there is no choice or pick to make. We use institutional asset class funds, which provide market return. Period. This is why we say MRP is the last investment strategy you will ever need.

Once investors have arrived at the conclusion that market return is what they need and want, the temptation to change their portfolio in uncertain times is eliminated. We have gone from the uncertainty of what move to make next to the relative certainty that we will receive market return. Furthermore, we can have full confidence that as long as free markets are in place, we will receive the full return of the market. It is there for the taking.

7 Chapter
Action Items

It is our sincerest hope that our message of simplicity, efficiency and logic has been an enlightening experience. The following action items are designed to give you a simple, usable list of what to do now. At the completion of these three steps, you are on your way to changing your financial life forever.

Step 1: Get the right help. Find a qualified advisory firm based on the questions and guidelines set forth in chapter 4. As we stated earlier—highly successful people rely on others who have gained expertise in their fields to help them achieve their goals. Don't be discouraged by the widespread mediocrity that exists in the financial services industry. An independent, direct pay, market return advisor is ready and willing to assist you.

The internet has made the task of finding one of these advisors much easier. You can visit www.paladinregistry.com or www.dfaus.com and click on the "Find an Advisor" link to begin your search.

Step 2: Create a written plan. Once the proper advisor is located, they will help you create a written financial plan which includes at minimum a retirement cash flow analysis and an investment policy statement. These written documents will allow you and your advisor to sustain a long-term strategy based on your specific goals and needs; not emotion. Whenever you become a little tense about markets, reviewing the plan allows you to regain your confidence in the free market system and reminds you why you made previous prudent decisions to allocate your investments in a certain way. It also allows you the comfort of staying in the market for the long haul.

Step 3: Diversify and own them all. It is now time to implement your plan by using institutional asset class funds in an MRP strategy. This will allow you to super-diversify and access the market return that is there for the taking in the MRP strategy.

The best time to super-diversify is always right now. If you have company stock in a 401(k) or think you are well-diversified simply because you have numerous individual securities or mutual funds, look closely. You don't want to make a costly mistake—especially now that you know better. Rely on the miracle of capitalism. You no longer have to be paralyzed with indecision because of market fluctuations. The best place for long-term investment dollars (five-plus years) is in the market. Hesitation smells of timing—not time in. Now that stock selection is a non-factor, you can own markets (not just stocks) and capture the capital market return that belongs to every investor—including you! This will allow free markets to work for you while you work (or play) at something else.

After these action steps are completed you will discover two very nice ancillary benefits:

You can now stop watching markets. By allowing markets to do the work, you can eliminate the time-consuming stressful activity of watching market ups and downs. This in turn allows you to avoid emotional mistakes that often accompany market-watching activity. Now that you understand that timing and picking decisions are futile anyway, what's the point?

You can do something more worthwhile. Consider all the time and energy that has now been freed up for really important things! Never again should you be a slave to market or economic news. This affords a great opportunity to reevaluate the things in life that are important to you and your family. It is time to get a new hobby, spend more time with loved ones, or get involved with a worthy cause.

TRACKING YOUR PORTFOLIO WITH THE MARKET RETURN BENCHMARK

When someone mentions the stock market, most people immediately think of the S&P 500 or maybe the Dow Jones Industrial Average. These familiar indexes have become synonymous with the market; even though, combined, they only represent approximately 12 percent of all US stocks. And that's not even considering international stocks, which make up 60 percent of the world's capital markets.

Indexes made sense fifty years ago because they were easy to calculate and follow. Although they were only relatively small samples of stocks, these indexes gave us a general indication of how the market had performed. Over the last five decades, however, investing has been revolutionized by the advent of computers and Modern Portfolio Theory. We now know that proper investing requires six to fifteen different asset classes. So why does the investing world insist on referring to only one or two indexes as "the market?"

A single index simply cannot tell the complete story of the stock market. Thinking in terms of a few indexes naturally encourages investors to make classic investing mistakes. They chase after the best-performing index because they are focusing on the individual components rather than a comprehensive portfolio. But it's the return of the entire portfolio that will determine whether your financial objectives will be achieved. Investors need a single benchmark for measuring the return of their portfolio, rather than piecemeal indexes telling only part of the story.

Amazingly, Wall Street has yet to create a true benchmark of the whole market for investors. Enter the Market Return Benchmark™.

The Market Return Benchmark provides a way to measure your portfolio return against the extended capital market system, which includes small and large US stocks, as well as small and large international stocks (including emerging markets). We created the Market Return Benchmark to include many asset classes, which are combined to represent the capital markets. (The Market Return Benchmark includes more than 13,000 equities in contrast to the thirty Dow Jones Industrial stocks or the stocks in the S&P 500 Index.) This is the new standard by which a portfolio should be measured—capital market return.

Investing has become much more of a science than an art. It's time we stopped using ancient, ineffective methods of investing (active management) and outdated tools for measuring success (indexes). The Market Return Benchmark focuses investors on a standard of measurement that reflects a market return philosophy and keeps the emphasis on the complete portfolio rather than the pieces. In short, indexes are created for money managers. The Market Return Benchmark is the first standard of measurement created for individual investors.

The Market Return Benchmark may be tracked at www.theinvestingrevolution.com. See Appendix C for composition.

Conclusion

In the introduction of this book, we stated that you may be asking questions such as: "Why haven't I heard of this before?" and "Why isn't everyone doing this?" We are still asking those same questions. Particularly when we consider that the fundamental principles of the MRP strategy, which are derived directly from Modern Portfolio Theory, have been taught in business schools around the country for decades. While you probably have already figured it out, we wanted to give you our answers to these two questions:

- The media thrive on newsworthy market volatility and uncertainty, which fosters active management habits among investors. Good market news and a market return strategy are considered boring.

- Major brokerage houses and financial firms are not in the business of educating the public. They are in the business of marketing products to the public.

- The politics and organizational structure of the financial services delivery system makes the dissemination and acceptance of MRP principles on a mass scale almost impossible. As Descartes once said, "A man is incapable of comprehending any argument that interferes with his revenue."

Our desire is that this information will in some way change the state of the industry that we believe needs major repair. Until then, our hope is that you have seen the advantages and wisdom of the Market Return Portfolio strategy. It is intended to deliver market return with market risk—and that only. There are no empty promises of beating the market or getting rich quick.

The MRP strategy is simply the best way to invest and thus benefit from the capitalist system that has made our country great. MRP is truly the last investment strategy you will ever need. You can now enjoy the peace of mind that comes from doing the right thing with your money. We expect to hear of your great accomplishments as you create wealth without worry!

A mind once stretched by a new idea never returns to its old dimensions.

–Oliver Wendell Holmes

Appendix A

Series include simulated and live returns. For portfolio construction, simulated data are used prior to the inception of the live portfolio. Simulated data do not reflect deduction of advisory fees, brokerage fees, and other expenses that a client would pay. Nor do simulated returns represent results of actual trading. Notations that follow identify which periods are simulated and which periods contain live data for each data series. Live data do not reflect the deduction of advisory fees, brokerage fees, and other expenses incurred by the portfolios. Live data incorporate actual trading results. Both simulated and live data reflect total returns.

Large cap market weighting allocated to US large company portfolio prior to August 1996 and allocated to S&P 500 Index prior to January 1991. Real estate stocks weighting allocated evenly between US micro cap portfolio and US small cap value portfolio prior to January 1975 data inception. International large cap value weighting allocated evenly between international small company portfolio and MSCI EAFE Index (net dividends) prior to January 1975 data inception. International small cap weighting allocated to international small company portfolio prior to January 1995 data inception. Emerging markets large, value, and small weighting allocated evenly between international value portfolio and international small company portfolio prior to data inception January 1987. Five-year global fixed income portfolio weighting allocated evenly between one-year fixed income portfolio, two-year global fixed income portfolio, and five-year government portfolio prior to January 1987 data inception.

US Equities

US MICRO CAP STOCKS

1926–1981: Deciles 9–10 NYSE1 (plus AMEX2 equivalents since July 1962 and NASDAQ3 equivalents since 1973). Courtesy of CRSP4. 1982–2003: US Micro Cap Portfolio net of all fees.

US SMALL CAP STOCKS

1926–May 1986: Deciles 6–10 NYSE (plus AMEX equivalents since July 1962 and NASDAQ equivalents since 1973). Courtesy of CRSP. June 1986–2003: US small cap trust net of administrative fees.

S&P 500 INDEX

© Stocks, Bonds, Bills, and Inflation 2003 Yearbook™, Ibbotson Associates, Chicago (annually updated work by Roger G. Ibbotson and Rex A. Sinquefield). Used with permission. All rights reserved.

US SMALL CAP VALUE STOCKS

1927–February 1992: Simulated strategy of lower-half market cap, upper 30 percent book-to-market NYSE (plus AMEX equivalents since July 1962 and NASDAQ equivalents since 1973). Courtesy of Fama/French and CRSP. March 1992–2003: US small cap value trust net of administrative fees.

US LARGE CAP VALUE STOCKS

1927–March 1993: Simulated strategy of upper-half market cap, upper 30 percent book-to-market NYSE (plus AMEX equivalents since July 1962 and NASDAQ equivalents since 1973). Courtesy of Fama/French and CRSP. Excludes utilities. April 1993–2003: US large value portfolio net of all fees.

US SMALL CAP GROWTH STOCKS

Simulated strategy of lower-half market cap, lower 30 percent book-to-market NYSE (plus AMEX equivalents since July 1962 and NASDAQ equivalents since 1973). Courtesy of Fama/French and CRSP.

US LARGE CAP GROWTH STOCKS

Simulated strategy of upper-half market cap, lower 30 percent book-to-market NYSE (plus AMEX equivalents since July 1962 and NASDAQ equivalents since 1973). Courtesy of Fama/French and CRSP. Excludes utilities.

US EQUITY REAL ESTATE INVESTMENT TRUSTS

1975–November 1994: Courtesy of Donald Keim, professor, Wharton School. Excludes healthcare REITs. December 1994–2003: Real estate securities portfolio net of all fees.

US SMALL CAP PORTFOLIO

1973–March 1992: Deciles 6-10 NYSE (plus AMEX equivalents since July 1962 and NASDAQ equivalents since 1973). Courtesy of CRSP. April 1992–2003: US small cap portfolio net of all fees.

US SMALL CAP VALUE PORTFOLIO

1973–March 1993: Simulated strategy of lower-half market cap, upper 30 percent book-to-market NYSE (plus AMEX and NASDAQ equivalents). Courtesy of Fama/French and CRSP. Excludes utilities. April 1993–2001: US small cap value portfolio net of all fees. Excludes utilities.

US LARGE COMPANY PORTFOLIO

1973–1990: S&P 500 Index. 1991–2003: US large company portfolio net of all fees.

ENHANCED US LARGE COMPANY PORTFOLIO

Enhanced US large company portfolio net of all fees.

Fixed Income

LONG-TERM GOVERNMENT BONDS

Average maturity: twenty years. © Stocks, Bonds, Bills, and Inflation 2003 Yearbook, Ibbotson Associates, Chicago (annually updated work by Roger G. Ibbotson and Rex A. Sinquefield). Used with permission. All rights reserved.

LONG-TERM CORPORATE BONDS

Average maturity: twenty years. © Stocks, Bonds, Bills, and Inflation 2003 Yearbook, Ibbotson Associates, Chicago (annually updated work by Roger G. Ibbotson and Rex A. Sinquefield). Used with permission. All rights reserved.

ONE-MONTH TREASURY BILLS

Average maturity: thirty days © Stocks, Bonds, Bills, and Inflation 2003 Yearbook, Ibbotson Associates, Chicago (annually updated work by Roger G. Ibbotson and Rex A. Sinquefield). Used with permission. All rights reserved.

ONE-MONTH CERTIFICATES OF DEPOSIT

1947–1971: One-month banker's acceptances. 1972–2003: One-month certificates of deposit.

ONE-YEAR FIXED INCOME STRATEGY

Average maturity: less than one year. 1972–July 1983: Simulated CD fixed income strategy (maximum maturity one year). August 1983–2003: One-year fixed income portfolio net of all fees.

FIVE-YEAR GOVERNMENT STRATEGY

Average maturity: Less than five years. 1953–May 1987: Simulation using US government instruments (maximum maturity five years). June 1987–2003: Five-year government portfolio net of all fees.

LEHMAN BROTHERS INTERMEDIATE GOVERNMENT/CREDIT BOND INDEX

Weighted average maturity: 3.5 - 4.5 years. Courtesy of Lehman Brothers Inc.

TWO-YEAR GLOBAL FIXED INCOME PORTFOLIO

Average maturity: two years or less. 1973–February 1996: Simulation using US government instruments (maximum maturity two years). March 1996–2003: Two-year global income portfolio net of all fees.

FIVE-YEAR GLOBAL FIXED INCOME PORTFOLIO

Average maturity: five years or less. 1987–November 1990: Lehman Hedged Country Indices: Equally weighted. US, U.K., Australia, Canada, Germany, France, Japan, Netherlands. Courtesy of Lehman Brothers Inc. December 1990–2003: Five-year global fixed income portfolio net of all fees.

International Equities

INTERNATIONAL SMALL CAP STOCKS AND INTERNATIONAL LARGE CAP STOCKS (COUNTRY WEIGHTS SAME FOR BOTH STRATEGIES)

1970–June 1988: 50 percent Japan, 50 percent United Kingdom. July 1988–September 1989: 50 percent Japan, 30 percent Continental, 20 percent United Kingdom. October 1989–March 1990: 40 percent Japan, 30 percent Continental, 20 percent United Kingdom, 10 percent Pacific Rim. April 1990–1992: 40 percent Japan, 35 percent Continental, 15 percent United Kingdom, 10 percent Pacific Rim. 1993–March 1997: 35 percent Japan, 35 percent Continental, 15 percent United Kingdom, 15 percent Pacific Rim. April 1997–March 1998: 30 percent Japan, 35 percent Continental, 15 percent United Kingdom, 20 percent Pacific Rim. April 1998–August 2000: 25 percent Japan, 40 percent Continental, 20 percent United Kingdom, 15 percent Pacific Rim. September 2000–March 2002: 35 percent Japan, 35 percent Continental, 15 percent United Kingdom, 15 percent Pacific Rim. April 2002–October 2003: 29 percent Japan, 42 percent Continental, 15 percent United Kingdom, 14 percent Pacific Rim. November 2003–December 2003: 27 percent Japan, 40 percent Continental, 20 percent United Kingdom, 13 percent Pacific Rim.

GLOBAL SMALL CAP STOCKS

1970–1986: 50 percent US small cap stocks, 50 percent international small cap stocks. 1987–2003: 50 percent US small cap stocks, 42.5 percent international small cap stocks, 7.5 percent emerging markets small cap stocks.

GLOBAL LARGE CAP STOCKS

1970–1986: 50 percent S&P Index, 50 percent international large cap stocks. 1987–2003: 50 percent S&P 500 Index, 42.5 percent international large cap stocks, 7.5 percent emerging markets stocks.

JAPAN SMALL CAP STOCKS

1970–March 1986: Smaller half of first section, Tokyo Stock Exchange. Courtesy of the Nomura Securities Investment Trust Management Company Ltd., Tokyo, rebalanced semiannually. April 1986–2003: Japanese small company portfolio net of all fees.

JAPAN LARGE CAP STOCKS

1970–June 1986: Larger half of first section, Tokyo Stock Exchange. Courtesy of the Nomura Securities Investment Trust Management Company Ltd., Tokyo. July 1986–2003: Japan Index, gross dividends reinvested (in US dollars). Courtesy of Morgan Stanley Capital International.

UNITED KINGDOM SMALL CAP STOCKS

1956–March 1986: Hoare Govett Smaller Companies Index. Courtesy London School of Business. April 1986–2003: United Kingdom small company portfolio net of all fees.

UNITED KINGDOM LARGE CAP STOCKS

FTSE All-Shares Index. Courtesy of FTSE.

CONTINENTAL SMALL CAP STOCKS

Countries presently include Austria, Belgium, Denmark, Finland, France, Germany, Greece, Ireland, Italy, the Netherlands, Norway, Portugal, Spain, Sweden, and Switzerland. Continental small company portfolio net of all fees.

CONTINENTAL LARGE CAP STOCKS

Europe excluding United Kingdom Index, gross dividends reinvested (in US dollars). Courtesy of Morgan Stanley Capital International.

PACIFIC RIM SMALL CAP STOCKS

Countries presently include Australia, Hong Kong, New Zealand, and Singapore. October 1989–1992: Pacific Rim small company trust net of administrative fees. 1993–2003: Pacific Rim small company portfolio net of all fees.

PACIFIC RIM LARGE CAP STOCKS

Pacific Rim excluding Japan Index, gross dividends reinvested (in US dollars). Courtesy of Morgan Stanley Capital International.

MSCI EAFE INDEX

Europe, Australia, and Far East Index. Courtesy of Morgan Stanley Capital International. Net dividends.

INTERNATIONAL VALUE STOCKS

1975–March 1993: Simulated value-weighted, unhedged strategy of stocks in Japan (maximum weight 38 percent), United Kingdom, Germany, France, the Netherlands, Belgium, Italy, Switzerland, Australia, and Hong Kong with over $500 million market cap and upper 30 percent book-to-market, returns in dollars. Courtesy of Fama/ French. April 1993–June 1993: MSCI EAFE Index substituted temporarily due to data availability. July 1993–February 1994: International high book-to-market portfolio net of all fees. March 1994–2003: International value portfolio net of all fees.

EMERGING MARKETS SMALL CAP STOCKS

Countries presently include Argentina, Brazil, Hungary, Indonesia, Israel, Malaysia, Mexico, Philippines, Poland, South Korea, Taiwan, Thailand, and Turkey. Equally weighted, rebalanced monthly. 1987–1996: Courtesy of Fama/French ("Value Versus Growth: The International Evidence." Journal of Finance 53 (1998), 1975–99.) 1997– February 1998: Emerging markets small cap series net of all fees. March 1998–2003: Emerging markets small cap portfolio net of all fees.

EMERGING MARKETS STOCKS

Chile is also included in the emerging markets strategy. 1987–February 1993: Courtesy of Fama/French ("Value Versus Growth: The International Evidence" Journal of Finance 53 (1998), 1975–99.) March 1993–May 1994: Emerging markets closed-end portfolio net of all fees. June 1994–2003: Emerging markets open-end portfolio net of all fees.

EMERGING MARKETS VALUE STOCKS

Chile is also included in the emerging markets value strategy. 1987–February 1993: Courtesy of Fama/French ("Value Versus Growth: The International Evidence." Journal of Finance 53 (1998), 1975–99.) March 1993–May 1994: Emerging markets closed-end portfolio net of all fees. June 1994–March 1998: Emerging Markets Value Fund Inc. April 1998–2003: Emerging markets value portfolio net of all fees.

INTERNATIONAL SMALL COMPANY PORTFOLIO

1970–September 1996: International small cap stocks. October 1996–2003: International small company portfolio net of all fees.

INTERNATIONAL SMALL CAP VALUE PORTFOLIO

International small cap value portfolio net of all fees.

INTERNATIONAL LARGE CAP PORTFOLIO

1973–July 1991: MSCI EAFE Index (net dividends). August 1991–2003: International large cap portfolio net of all fees.

Inflation

INFLATION: CHANGES IN THE CONSUMER PRICE INDEX

© Stocks, Bonds, Bills, and Inflation 2003 Yearbook, Ibbotson Associates, Chicago (annually updated work by Roger G. Ibbotson and Rex A. Sinquefield). Used with permission. All rights reserved.
1 NYSE: New York Stock Exchange
2 AMEX: American Stock Exchange
3 NASDAQ: NASDAQ National Market System
4 CRSP: Center for Research in Security Prices, University of Chicago

*Appendix A source: Dimensional Fund
Advisors Matrix Book 2003.*

Appendix B

Year	F/F Lrg Val Index	F/F Lrg Co. Index	F/F Lrg Gro Index	F/F Sml Val Index	F/F Sml Co. Index	F/F Sml Gro Index	One Month T-Bills	Five Year T-Notes	Long-term Gov't Bonds	Long-term Corp. Bonds
1927	31.25	22.93	46.18	35.29	25	31.42	3.13	4.51	8.94	7.44
1928	23.63	31.87	48.05	40.96	39.64	34.86	3.23	0.92	0.08	2.84
1929	-3.93	0.27	-21.07	-35.77	-30.78	-44.23	4.74	6.02	3.42	3.27
1930	-43.16	-29.32	-26.44	-46.38	-31.23	-35.85	2.43	6.72	4.65	7.98
1931	-58.24	-60.13	-36.96	-51.87	-47.4	-42.7	1.09	-2.31	-5.32	-1.85
1932	-3.26	-15.61	-7.93	1.35	-10.26	-5.25	0.95	8.81	16.84	10.82
1933	116.91	90.03	44.65	118.69	125.63	159.41	0.3	1.83	-0.07	10.38
1934	-21.51	-3.25	11.06	8.51	18.25	35.89	0.18	9	10.01	13.84
1935	51.14	47.15	42.22	53.16	76.69	48.34	0.14	6.99	5	9.61
1936	48.12	38.25	26.46	73.19	48.92	37.1	0.19	3.04	7.5	6.74
1937	-41.07	-31.91	-34.12	-51.47	-48.74	-48.64	0.29	1.57	0.22	2.75
1938	25.2	20.04	33.2	26.21	43.39	43.81	-0.04	6.23	5.51	6.13
1939	-12.51	-3.22	7.73	-3.55	0.7	10.72	0.01	4.52	5.95	3.97
1940	-2.62	-2.78	-9.81	-9.83	-1.82	0.57	-0.02	2.96	6.09	3.39
1941	-0.88	-4.72	-12.67	-4.82	-10.96	-17.34	0.04	0.49	0.93	2.73
1942	33.71	17.48	13.17	35	29.2	16.76	0.28	1.92	3.22	2.6
1943	44.02	34	22.04	91.82	55.09	45.08	0.35	2.8	2.07	2.83
1944	41.98	22.27	16.11	49.71	40.12	41.23	0.33	1.81	2.82	4.73
1945	49.06	38.87	31.95	74.61	59.73	64.28	0.32	2.21	10.73	4.08
1946	-8.29	-1.41	-8.29	-7.36	-10.26	-12.4	0.36	1.01	-0.09	1.72
1947	8.66	4.25	4.1	5.34	-2.49	-8.38	0.5	0.92	-2.63	-2.34
1948	5.09	1.59	3.35	-2.3	-7.43	-7.16	0.81	1.86	3.39	4.14
1949	18.71	16.1	23.31	21.04	23.05	23.52	1.12	2.33	6.44	3.31
1950	55.22	31.08	23.11	52.16	32.26	31.01	1.22	0.7	0.05	2.12
1951	14.36	24.78	20.05	12.27	15.74	16.26	1.49	0.36	-3.94	-2.69

Year	F/F Lrg Val Index	F/F Lrg Co. Index	F/F Lrg Gro Index	F/F Sml Val Index	F/F Sml Co. Index	F/F Sml Gro Index	One Month T-Bills	Five Year T-Notes	Long-term Gov't Bonds	Long-term Corp. Bonds
1952	19.54	13.34	13.38	8.59	9.46	8.55	1.65	1.63	1.16	3.52
1953	-7.04	0.24	2.29	-6.92	-0.97	-0.68	1.83	3.23	3.63	3.41
1954	77.32	48.13	47.79	63.43	60.77	43.2	0.86	2.7	7.18	5.39
1955	29.78	18.85	28.5	23.47	20.95	13.95	1.57	-0.66	-1.28	0.48
1956	3.37	12.97	6.52	5.98	7.21	7.65	2.47	-0.42	-5.58	-6.81
1957	-22.72	-8.23	-9.14	-15.9	-14.52	-16.99	3.15	7.84	7.47	8.71
1958	72.3	45.34	41.62	69.67	57.18	75.22	1.53	-1.3	-6.11	-2.22
1959	18.82	9.66	13.15	17.42	19.72	21.42	2.97	-0.38	-2.28	-0.97
1960	-8.56	8.57	-2.36	-6.02	-1.78	-1.78	2.67	11.75	13.79	9.07
1961	28.89	26.73	26.43	30.85	30.27	22.2	2.12	1.87	0.96	4.82
1962	-3.09	-5.46	-10.89	-9.47	-15.37	-22.33	2.72	5.58	6.88	7.95
1963	32.35	17.07	21.88	28.34	16.72	7.98	3.11	1.64	1.21	2.19
1964	19.16	20.28	14.48	22.9	17.54	8.13	3.53	4.03	3.51	4.77
1965	22.42	10.08	13.36	42.5	31.84	39.99	3.92	1.01	0.7	-0.46
1966	-10.21	-6.11	-10.77	-7.76	-5.67	-5.32	4.75	4.68	3.65	0.2
1967	31.74	15.92	29.17	67.55	72.71	88.42	4.2	1	-9.19	-4.95
1968	27.08	15.86	4.03	45.81	41.11	32.73	5.22	4.53	-0.26	2.57
1969	-16.39	-16.75	2.88	-25.84	-22.71	-23.68	6.57	-0.74	-5.07	-8.09
1970	10.63	8.12	-5.65	6.62	-7.7	-20.25	6.52	16.85	12.1	18.37
1971	12.55	6.15	23.94	14.47	21.1	25.86	4.39	8.74	13.24	11.01
1972	18.62	11.21	21.32	7.28	6.76	0.39	3.84	5.17	5.67	7.26
1973	-3.67	-8.66	-21.79	-27.23	-33.62	-45.07	6.93	4.61	-1.1	1.14
1974	-23.4	-22.95	-29.24	-19.02	-26.49	-31.9	8.01	5.68	4.35	-3.06
1975	55.9	41.92	34.44	57.12	58.94	61.32	5.8	7.82	9.19	14.64
1976	44.62	41.01	17.54	59.13	47.23	38.2	5.08	12.88	16.76	18.65
1977	1.64	-0.76	-9.46	23.82	17.96	19.35	5.13	1.4	-0.65	1.71
1978	3.48	6.73	7	22.12	19.93	17.65	7.2	3.49	-1.18	-0.07
1979	22.67	23.39	16.59	38.33	36.69	48.84	10.38	4.1	-1.21	-4.19
1980	16.45	37.54	35.2	22.28	31	52.66	11.26	3.9	-3.96	-2.61
1981	12.8	-7.62	-7.13	17.68	13.8	-11.53	14.72	9.44	1.86	-0.96
1982	27.67	17.41	21.48	39.86	33.35	19.72	10.53	29.1	40.37	43.79
1983	26.92	24.97	14.67	47.58	38.69	22.12	8.8	7.41	0.69	4.7
1984	16.17	5.67	-0.72	7.52	0.6	-12.84	9.78	14.03	15.54	16.39
1985	31.75	32.01	32.64	32.12	32.61	28.91	7.73	20.34	30.96	30.9

Year	F/F Lrg Val Index	F/F Lrg Co. Index	F/F Lrg Gro Index	F/F Sml Val Index	F/F Sml Co. Index	F/F Sml Gro Index	One Month T-Bills	Five Year T-Notes	Long-term Gov't Bonds	Long-term Corp. Bonds
1986	21.82	20.65	14.38	14.5	10.41	1.95	6.15	15.13	24.45	19.85
1987	-2.76	3.25	7.43	-7.12	-3.88	-12.24	5.46	2.9	-2.7	-0.27
1988	25.96	17.53	12.53	30.76	28.78	16.63	6.36	6.09	9.68	10.7
1989	29.7	24.63	36.11	15.7	18.13	20.58	8.38	13.27	18.1	16.23
1990	-12.75	-5.62	1.06	-25.13	-17.65	-17.74	7.82	9.74	6.2	6.78
1991	27.35	22.14	43.33	40.56	47.04	54.73	5.6	15.31	19.26	19.89
1992	23.57	9.65	6.41	34.76	22.4	5.82	3.5	7.2	9.41	9.39
1993	19.51	16.13	2.38	29.41	18.41	12.64	2.9	11.24	18.24	13.19
1994	-5.78	0.09	1.95	3.21	-1.41	-4.36	3.91	-5.13	-7.78	-7.03
1995	37.68	36.74	37.16	27.69	27.95	35.13	5.6	16.11	31.67	26.39
1996	13.35	26.3	21.25	20.71	22.24	12.36	5.2	2.09	-0.92	1.4
1997	31.88	32.28	31.61	37.29	32.01	15.29	5.25	8.38	15.87	12.95
1998	16.23	9.23	34.64	-8.63	-4.19	3.04	4.85	10.22	13.07	10.76
1999	-0.22	7.51	29.43	5.59	11.37	54.75	4.69	-1.76	-8.99	-7.45
2000	5.8	4.62	-13.63	-0.8	4.67	-24.15	5.88	12.6	21.49	12.85
2001	-1.18	-1.85	-15.59	40.24	26.2	0.16	3.85	7.61	3.7	10.65
2002	-32.53	-15.89	-21.5	-12.41	-13.57	-30.87	1.63	12.95	17.-	16.33
2003	35.07	33.85	26.29	74.69	51.56	53.2	1.02	2.4	1.44	5.27
2004	18.91	17.21	6.53	26.59	22.48	12.54	1.19	3.2	9.34	8.72

Source: Dimensional Fund Advisors. F/F is Fama/French.
Eugene Fama, University of Chicago; Kenneth French, MIT.

Appendix C

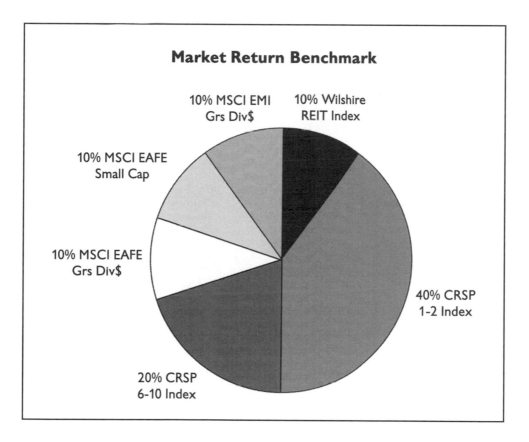

Market Return Benchmark

- 10% MSCI EMI Grs Div$
- 10% Wilshire REIT Index
- 10% MSCI EAFE Small Cap
- 10% MSCI EAFE Grs Div$
- 40% CRSP 1-2 Index
- 20% CRSP 6-10 Index

Description of asset classes used in Market Return Benchmark

Index	Asset Class
CRSP 1-2 Index	Large Cap US
CRSP 6-10 Index	Small Cap US
Wilshire REIT Index	Real Estate Investment Trusts
MSCI EAFE	International
MSCI EAFE Small Company	International Small Cap
MSCI Emerging Markets Index	Emerging Markets

CRSP—Capital Research in Security Prices, University of Chicago

MSCI—Morgan Stanley Capital International

*The Market Return Benchmark is NOT an investment product. You CANNOT invest in the benchmark directly.

The Market Return Benchmark is designed to be used as an educational tool that will allow investors to measure the performance of their portfolio against a diversified 100% equity portfolio representing exposure to multiple asset classes.

This information should not be construed as an offer to sell or buy any investment product or as specific advice to any individual.

Notes

Chapter 1

1. "Privileged Information from Peter Lynch, The Biggest Mistakes to Avoid Now," *The Bottom Line*, March 1, 1994.
2. Burton Malkiel, *A Random Walk Down Wall Street* (New York, W.W. Norton, 1996), p. 186.
3. http://www.twainquotes.com/Lies.html. The quote "There are three kinds of lies: lies, damned lies, and statistics" is more likely from Leonard Courtney.
4. David Dreman, *Contrarian Investment Strategy: The Psychology of Stock Market Success* (New York, Random House, 1979).
5. Standard & Poor's is a division of The McGraw-Hill Companies Inc.
6. Data Source: MSN Money
7. Ibid.
8. Remarks by Federal Reserve Chairman Alan Greenspan at the Annual Dinner and Francis Boyer Lecture of The American Enterprise Institute for Public Policy Research. Mr. Greenspan's speech was titled "The Challenge of Central Banking in a Democratic Society."
http://www.federalreserve.gov/boarddocs/speeches/1996/19961205.htm.
9. Source: Dimensional Fund Advisors
10. Morningstar Principia Pro Database, December 2003. Includes only mutual funds with 85 percent or more in US equity holdings, excluding index funds and funds that do not have an annualized ten-year return. Distinct portfolios only.
11. Ibid.

Chapter 2

1. Paul Asquith, Michael Mikhail, and Andrea Ai, "The Information in Equity Analyst Reports." National Bureau of Economic Research. http://www.nber.org/digest/apr03/w9246.html.
2. Berkshire Hathaway 2003 Annual Report, pp. 2, 5.
3. Morningstar Principia Database, December 2004.
4. Morningstar Principia Pro Database, December 2004. Includes only mutual funds with 85 percent or more in US equity holdings and that fall within the large portion of Morningstar's style box. Excludes index funds and those that do not have a ten-year annualized return. Distinct portfolios only.
5. David Rynecki, "Ten Stocks to Last a Decade," *Fortune*, August 14, 2000.
6. Morningstar Principia Pro Database, December 2004.
7. Ibid.
8. The Equity Market Return Portfolio is composed of funds managed by Dimensional Fund Advisors (DFA). The composition of the portfolio model is detailed below:

Equity Portfolio	Percentage
DFA Enhanced US Large Company	20%
DFA US Large Cap Value	20%
DFA US Micro Cap	10%
DFA US Small Cap Value	10%
DFA Real Estate Securities	10%
DFA International Value	10%
DFA International Small Company	5%
DFA International Small Cap Value	5%
DFA Emerging Markets	3%
DFA Emerging Markets Value	3%
DFA Emerging Markets Small Cap	4%

See Appendix A for additional portfolio composition information.

9. Marion Asnes, Peter Carbonara, et al., "Money 100—The Best 100 Mutual Funds—The Only List You Need," *Money*, June 1999.
10. Data source: Morningstar Principia Pro Database, December 2003, and CNN Money.

11. Funds A, B, C, and D are actual funds. They are not identified because the purpose of this illustration is not to sell a particular security. It is to emphasize that ratings, in and of themselves, do not provide enough information for making an investment decision. Funds were analyzed in December 2000 and January 2001.

12. Ian McDonald, "Mutual-Fund Expenses Keep Rising—Despite Trading Probes, Firms Post Better Profits, Helped by Increasing Fees," Wall Street Journal Online, November 3, 2003.

13. Morningstar Principia Pro Database, December 2004. Selection criteria include only actively managed equity mutual funds.

14. Morningstar Principia Pro Database, December 2004. Selection criteria include only Dimensional Fund Advisor funds.

15. Judith Burns, "Investors May Get Better Cost View, SEC Is Readying Proposal to Provide More Clarity on Fund Trading Expenses," *The Wall Street Journal*, Pg. C15, January 31, 2005.

Chapter 3

1. See Appendix B.

2. Arthur Levitt, *Take on the Street* (New York, Pantheon, 2002), p. 56.

3. US Securities and Exchange Commission, Division of Investment Management: Report on Mutual Fund Fees and Expenses, December 2000. http://www.sec. gov/news/studies/feestudy.htm.
   Carhart, Mark M., 1997, "On Persistence in Mutual Fund Performance," *Journal of Finance*, pp. 52, 57–82.

4. Morningstar Principia Pro Database, December 2003. Includes only mutual funds with 85 percent or more in US equity holdings, excluding index funds and DFA funds. Distinct portfolios only.

5. Morningstar Principia Pro Database as of December 31, 2004.

6. Yuka Hayash, "Funds Closed at Brisk Pace in 2003," Wall Street Journal Online, March 4, 2004.

7. Includes funds having minimum assets of $100 million at the end of 1996 (851 funds).

8. For example, the NBA Eastern Conference franchises had replaced fourteen of fifteen head coaches halfway through the 2003–2004 season.

9. The fund being described is the Fidelity Magellan Fund.

10. Morningstar Principia Pro Database, December 2004. Includes only actively managed equity mutual funds. This excludes index funds, enhanced index funds, DFA funds and exchange-traded funds (ETFs).

11. Einstein was quoting Benjamin Franklin.

12. Henry Blodget, "Streetwise: A scandal waiting to happen," *Euromoney Magazine*, December, 2004.

Chapter 4

1. Senator Carter Glass (D-Va.) and Congressman Henry Steagall (D-Ala.) introduced legislation in 1933, in the midst of the Depression, that sought to separate commercial banking and securities underwriting (brokerage services). The law eventually became known as the Glass-Steagall Act of 1933. It was designed to prevent the conflicts of interests that supposedly arose when commercial banks provided banking and investment services to the public. Additional limits on the activities of banks and bank holding companies were enacted in 1956 with the passage of the Bank Holding Company Act. Under this act, banks and bank holding companies were prevented from offering nonbanking services such as providing insurance. This legislation was an effort to control the growing trend toward financial services conglomerates. In April 1998, sixty-five years after the passage of Glass-Steagall, Travelers Corporation and Citicorp announced the world's largest merger—today's Citigroup. At the time the two companies provided services that included banking, brokerage and insurance. Congress paved the way for this merger eighteen months later with the passage of the Financial Services Modernization Act of 1999, effectively repealing Glass-Steagall. http://www.sia.com/capitol_hill/html/glass-steagall_act.html and http://banking.senate.gov/conf/somfinal.htm.

2. Daniel Solin, *Does Your Broker Owe You Money?* (Indianapolis, Alpha, 2003), p. 232.

3. Arthur Levitt, *Take on the Street* (New York, Pantheon, 2002), p. 312.

4. http://www.brainyquote.com/quotes/authors/v/vernon_law.html.

5. Thomas Spinelli and Margaret Honan, "Recruiting Pressures Grow," The National Underwriter Company, March 22, 2004.

Chapter 5

1. Data source: Dimensional Fund Advisors. A bear market was categorized as a 20 percent or more drop in the S&P 500 Index. From 1926 to 2004 there have been thirteen bear markets.

Time Period	S&P 500
9-29 to 11-29	-33.08%
4-30 to 6-32	-79.570%
8-32 to 2-33	29.82%
2-34 to 7-34	-20.70%
3-37 to 3-38	-50.04%
10-39 to 5-40	-25.72%
9-41 to 4-42	-22.39%
6-46 to 4-47	-20.96%
1-62 to 6-62	-22.28%
12-68 to 6-70	-29.23%
1-73 to 9-74	-42.62%
9-87 to 11-87	-29.53%
9-00 to 9-02	-44.73%

Bull (nonbear) market periods for the S&P 500 Index from 1926 to 2004:

Time Period	S&P 500
1-26 to 8-29	193.29%
12-29 to 3-30	21.40%
7-32 to 8-32	91.60%
3-33 to 1-34	105.35%
8-34 to 2-37	135.14%
4-38 to 9-39	64.68%
6-40 to 8-41	20.95%
5-42 to 5-46	209.84%
5-47 to 12-61	925.44%
7-62 to 11-68	143.85%
7-70 to 12-72	75.60%
10-74 to 8-87	843.64%
12-87 to 8-00	814.15%
10-02 to 12-04	54.72%

2. Data source: Dimensional Fund Advisors.

3. Ibid.

4. Ibid.

5. Interest rates were taken from February 1980 and February 2000. Inflation CPI Data source: Dimensional Fund Advisors. http://research.stlouisfed.org/fred2/data/TB1YA.txt.

6. S&P 500 Index represents large cap stocks. CRSP (Center for Research in Securities Pricing, University of Chicago) deciles 6-10 represent small cap stocks.

7. Data source: Dimensional Fund Advisors.

8. Weston Wellington, "Lessons of 2003," Dimensional Fund Advisors, March 2004.

9. S&P 500 represents large cap stocks. The CRSP deciles 9–10 represent small cap stocks. International stocks are represented by the MSCI EAFE (Morgan Stanley Capital International Europe Australia and the Far East).

10. Morningstar Principia Pro Database, December 2004. The universe of funds was filtered as described below:

    (a) Large blend funds—includes stock funds with 85 percent or more in US companies that fall in Morningstar's large growth category. Excludes index funds, enhanced index funds and DFA funds. Distinct portfolio only. Large blend funds were compared against the S&P 500 Index.

    (b) Large value funds—includes stock funds with 85 percent or more in US companies that fall in Morningstar's large value category. Excludes index funds, enhanced index funds and DFA funds. Distinct portfolio only. Large value funds were compared against the Russell 1000 Value Index.

    (c) Small value funds—includes stock funds with 85 percent or more in US companies that fall in Morningstar's small value category. Excludes index funds, enhanced index funds and DFA funds. Distinct portfolio only. Small value funds were compared against the Russell 2000 Value Index.

    (d) International funds—includes stock funds that fall into Morningstar's prospectus objective as foreign stock and fall into Morningstar's style box as large cap. Excludes index funds, enhanced index funds and DFA funds. Distinct portfolio only. International funds were compared against the MSCI EAFE Index.

11. Bud Carter, "Chairman Carter's Collection of Pithy Quotes," 2003, p. 19.

12. See note 10. Beta filter equal to or less than 1.0 was added to previous category filters. Data source: Morningstar Principia Pro Database, December 2004.

13. The Equity, Aggressive, and Balanced Market Return Portfolios are comprised of funds managed by Dimensional Fund Advisors. The composition of the portfolios is detailed in the following tables:

Equity Portfolio	Percentage
DFA Enhanced US Large Company	20%
DFA US Large Cap Value	20%
DFA US Micro Cap	10%
DFA US Small Cap Value	10%
DFA Real Estate Securities	10%
DFA International Value	10%
DFA International Small Company	5%
DFA International Small Cap Value	5%
DFA Emerging Markets	3%
DFA Emerging Markets Value	3%
DFA Emerging Markets Small Cap	4%

Aggressive Portfolio	Percentage
DFA Enhanced US Large Company	16%
DFA US Large Cap Value	16%
DFA US Micro Cap	8%
DFA US Small Cap Value	8%
DFA Real Estate Securities	8%
DFA International Value	8%
DFA International Small Company	4%
DFA International Small Cap Value	4%
DFA Emerging Markets	2.4%
DFA Emerging Markets Value	2.4%
DFA Emerging Markets Small Cap	3.2%
DFA One-Year Fixed Income	5%
DFA Two-Year Global Fixed Income	5%
DFA Five-Year Government	5%
DFA Five-Year Global Fixed Income	5%

Balanced Portfolio	Percentage
DFA Enhanced US Large Company	12%
DFA US Large Cap Value	12%
DFA US Micro Cap	6%
DFA US Small Cap Value	6%
DFA Real Estate Securities	6%
DFA International Value	6%
DFA International Small Company	3%
DFA International Small Cap Value	3%
DFA Emerging Markets	1.8%
DFA Emerging Markets Value	1.8%
DFA Emerging Markets Small Cap	2.4%
DFA One-Year Fixed Income	10%
DFA Two-Year Global Fixed Income	10%
DFA Five-Year Government	10%
DFA Five-Year Global Fixed Income	10%

See Appendix A for additional portfolio composition information.

14. Ibid.
15. Ibid.
16. Ibid.
17. Ibid.
18. Morningstar Principia Pro Database, December 2004. The universe of funds was filtered as described below:
   (a) Large cap funds—includes stock funds with 85 percent or more in US companies that fall in Morningstar's large style box. Excludes index funds, enhanced index funds, DFA funds and funds that did not have year 2000 returns. Distinct portfolio only; 820 funds.
   (b) Mid cap funds—includes stock funds with 85 percent or more in US companies that fall in Morningstar's mid cap style box. Excludes index funds, enhanced index funds, DFA funds and funds that did not have year 2000 returns. Distinct portfolio only; 375 funds.
   (c) Small cap funds—includes stock funds with 85 percent or more in US companies that fall in Morningstar's small style box. Excludes index funds, enhanced index funds, DFA funds, and funds that did not have year 2000 returns. Distinct portfolio only; 317 funds.

A scheduled portfolio was prepared in Morningstar Principia Pro for each of the above categories using a time frame of March 1, 2000, to December 31, 2004. With a total of 1,512 funds used, a weighted return was applied to each category and then summarized.

19. Data Source: Dimensional Fund Advisors; Morningstar Principia Pro; Dow Jones. See also note 13.

20. See note 13.

21. See note 13.

22. See note 13.

Chapter 6

1. Matthew 7:24-27.

2. http://www.holland.nl/uk/holland/sights/tulips-history.html.

3. Harry Markowitz, "Portfolio Selection," *The Journal of Finance,* March 1952, pp. 77-91.

   His work was first published while he was still in graduate school at the University of Chicago. Markowitz proposed that you could build a diversified portfolio that would lower risk as well as provide higher returns because of the benefits of diversification. According to his theory, investors can build optimal portfolios that maximize expected return for any level of market risk. The research in portfolio construction that has evolved from the 1952 paper by Markowitz is known as Modern Portfolio Theory.

4. Discussion of institutional asset class fund characteristics derived from more detailed discussion on pages 70-76 in *The Prudent Investor's Guide to Beating Wall Street at Its Own Game,* John J. Bowen, Jr. & Daniel C. Goldie. McGraw-Hill: New York, 1998.

5. Institutional asset class funds are traditional open-ended mutual funds. Open-ended mutual fund investors can purchase or sell shares during trading hours and receive that evening's closing price. Cash from the sale of a mutual fund is made available upon settlement of the trade based on Federal Reserve guidelines.

6. See chapter 2, note 13.

7. See chapter 2, note 14.

8. See chapter 3, note 10.

9. The fund management team uses objective criteria based on academic research. For example, in the small US company category, small companies are defined as those whose market capitalization (price x shares outstanding) comprises the smallest, 12.5 percent, of the total market universe. The total market universe

is defined as the aggregate capitalization of the NYSE, AMEX, and NASDAQ National Market System companies. They also employ additional screening criteria. These criteria include eliminating REITs, closed-end investment companies, limited partnerships, companies in bankruptcy, ADRs, companies with qualified financial statements, OTC stocks with fewer than four market makers, and those not included in the National Market System. They are aggressive in keeping cash levels low, generally under 2 percent. New cash flow is controlled so portfolios may remain fully invested. On at least a semiannual basis, the market capitalization ranking of eligible stocks is examined to determine which issues are eligible for purchase and which are sale candidates. A hold or buffer range for sales minimizes transaction costs and keeps portfolio turnover low. Issues that migrate above the hold range are sold and proceeds reinvested in the portfolio.

10. Morningstar Principia Pro Database, December 2004. Selection criteria include only equity Dimensional Funds contained in the 80:20 model (See note 13).

11. Gary Brinson, Randolph Hood and Gilbert Beebower, "Determinants of Portfolio Performance," Financial Analyst Journal, July-August 1986, pp. 39-44.

12. The diversified index portfolio (DIP) is an 80:20 stock-to-bond ratio. S&P 500 Index represents large cap stocks; Russell 2000 Index represents small cap stocks; MSCI EAFE Index represents international stocks; Lehman Brothers Intermediate Government/Credit Index represents fixed income holdings. Data Source: Dimensional Fund Advisors.

13. The 80:20 Market Return Portfolio is composed of funds managed by Dimensional Fund Advisors. The composition of the portfolio is detailed on the next page.

80:20 Portfolio	Percentage
DFA Enhanced US Large Company	16%
DFA US Large Cap Value	16%
DFA US Micro Cap	8%
DFA US Small Cap Value	8%
DFA Real Estate Securities	8%
DFA International Value	8%
DFA International Small Company	4%
DFA International Small Cap Value	4%
DFA Emerging Markets	2.4%
DFA Emerging Markets Value	2.4%
DFA Emerging Markets Small Cap	3.2%
DFA One-Year Fixed Income	5%
DFA Two-Year Global Fixed Income	5%
DFA Five-Year Government	5%
DFA Five-Year Global Fixed Income	5%

See Appendix A for additional portfolio composition information.

14. Data Source: Dimensional Fund Advisors.
15. Lynch, Anthony, and Richard Mendenhall, "New Evidence on Stock Price Effects Associated With Changes in the S&P 500 Index," *Journal of Business* 70 (1997): 351-83.
16. Chakrabarti, Rajesh, Wei Huang, Narayanan Jayaraman, and Jinsoo Lee, "Do International Investors' Demand Curves for Stocks Slope Down Too?," working paper.
17. Ananth Mahavan, "The Russell Reconstitution Effect," *Financial Analyst Journal.* July-August 2003 and Peter Jankovskis, "The Not-So-Perfect Index," *Journal of Indexes,* Second Quarter 2002.

18. Number of holdings is as of December 31, 2004.

Portfolio Name	# of Holdings
DFA US Large Company	497
DFA US Large Cap Value	225
DFA US Micro Cap	2494
DFA US Small Cap Value	1391
DFA Real Estate Securities	126
DFA International Value	577
DFA International Small Company	4240
DFA International Small Cap Value	2459
DFA Emerging Markets	535
DFA Emerging Markets Value	1335
DFA Emerging Markets Small Cap	1308
Index	# of Holdings
S&P 500 Index	500
Russell 2000 Index	2022
MSCI EAFE Index	1064

19. Data Source: Dimensional Fund Advisors.

20. John Bowen and Daniel Goldie, *The Prudent Investor's Guide to Beating Wall Street at Its Own Game* (New York, McGraw-Hill, 1998), p. 99.

    Bowen and Goldie cite as an example the returns of Colgate-Palmolive Inc., which receives "about 80 percent of its revenues from foreign operations, yet its stock price still closely followed the US market during a period when foreign markets significantly underperformed [1992–1997]. Because stocks of US multinational firms are so highly correlated with the US market, they lose their diversification power. To capture the diversification benefits of foreign equities, you must purchase shares of companies headquartered in foreign countries."

21. Annualized returns. Data Source: Dimensional Fund Advisors Matrix Book 2004.

Index Name	Return (1984-1989)
S&P 500	17.9%
Japan Large Cap	36.1%
Global Large Cap	25.4%

22. Large cap and small cap indices are from Fama/French data. Eugene Fama, University of Chicago; Kenneth French, MIT. EAFE is Morgan Stanley Capital International Europe, Australia, and the Far East Index. Data Source: Dimensional Fund Advisors.

23. Rankings are based on standard deviation. Data Source: Dimensional Fund Advisors.

24. http://www.ssa.gov/OACT/TR/TR05/tr05.pdf.

25. Transcript of John Bogle statement before the United States Senate Committee on Banking, Housing, and Urban Affairs, February 26, 2004, p. 9.

Reading List

Wealth Without Worry was written for the general reader who may have limited knowledge about the world of finance. We purposely kept to the central key points that could change a reader's paradigm about investing and left out most discussions of the research and data. If you now have a newfound interest in investing or Modern Portfolio Theory then you should explore some of the books on the list below.

1. Belsky, Gary, and Thomas Gilovich. *Why Smart People Make Big Money Mistakes and How to Correct Them.* Simon & Schuster: New York, 1999.

2. Bernstein, Peter L. *Against the Gods.* John Wiley & Sons Inc.: New York, 1996.

3. Bernstein, William. *The Four Pillars of Investing.* McGraw-Hill: New York, 2002.

4. Bogle, John. *Bogle on Mutual Funds.* McGraw-Hill: New York, 1993.

5. Bowen, John J., and Daniel C. Goldie. *The Prudent Investor's Guide to Beating Wall Street at Its Own Game.* McGraw-Hill: New York, 1998.

6. Carter, Marshall N., and William G. Shipman. *Promises to Keep, Saving Social Security's Dream.* Regnery Publishing Inc.: Washington, D.C., 1996.

7. Ellis, Charles. *Investment Policy, How to Win the Losers Game.* Irwin Professional Publishing: Chicago, 1993.

8. Kotlikoff, Laurence J., and Scott Burns. *The Coming Generational Storm.* The MIT Press: Cambridge, Massachusetts, 2004.

9. Levitt, Arthur. *Take on the Street.* Pantheon Books: New York, 2002.

10. Malkiel, Burton. *A Random Walk Down Wall Street.* W.W. Norton & Company: New York, 1996.

11. Ross, Ron. *The Unbeatable Market.* Bookmasters Inc.: Mansfield, Ohio, 2002.

12. Solin, Daniel R. *Does Your Broker Owe You Money?* Alpha Books: Indianapolis, 2003.

13. Waymire, Jack. *Who's Watching Your Money?* John Wiley & Sons, Inc. Hoboken, New Jersey, 2004.

G
Glossary

1:1. The idea (actually a truism), expressed as a ratio, that a portfolio invested in the entire equity market will achieve a return that is equal to the total market with a probability of 100 percent—a one-in-one chance. Actual portfolios can only approximate a total market portfolio and, consequently, may not achieve returns exactly equal to market return. The goal, however, is to earn market return as close to 1:1 as possible.

active management. The system of investment management that is dependent on successfully predicting market and security movements (timing) and security selection (picking).

active marketing. The marketing by the financial services establishment that tends to promote emotional decisions by consumers.

direct pay. Money paid exclusively from a client, directly to an advisory firm for financial advice. Direct pay is different from the entrenched Wall Street system of indirect payments, subsidies, and sales commissions.

efficient analyst paradox. Logical conclusion that the work of many highly skilled securities analysts will ensure efficient market prices, thus making those same skilled analysts unable to consistently find undervalued stocks.

extended market. The exposure afforded by the additional securities present in a market return strategy above and beyond normal portfolio composition. (The MRP may hold as many as 15,000 to 16,000 individual securities.)

facilitators. Representatives from the financial services industry who offer products that tend to appeal to investor emotions rather than investor needs.

fiduciary. Advisors acting in the best interests of their client and disclosing any real or implied conflicts of interest. This is generally a higher standard than is customary in the financial services industry.

fiduciary organizational intelligence. The collective knowledge and resources applied to an advisor/client relationship by a firm working as a unit or team devoted to the client's best interests in a fiduciary manner.

giant portfolio stop-loss effect. Beneficial effect caused by the superdiversification found in a Market Return Portfolio, which tends to limit volatility during down markets.

inalienable wealth. The concept which allows that the prosperity which is freely available via capital markets is incapable of being alienated, surrendered, transferred, or otherwise forfeited without the consent of a free market participant. An investor gives up the right to inalienable wealth when he/she knowingly or unknowingly succumbs to the tyrannical Wall Street financial complex and its failed methodologies.

independent advisor. Advisor who is not employed or related in any way to brokerage houses, banks or other financial institutions that may profit from offering incentives to advisors for recommending particular products. An independent advisor will be associated with a fee-based Registered Investment Advisor (RIA).

institutional asset class funds. Low-cost no-load mutual funds designed to represent whole asset classes as defined by Modern Portfolio Theory. Characteristically, they maintain their asset class integrity so that diversification remains dependable. These funds are used by large institutional investors (such as pension and scholarship funds) and by the clients of many independent advisors.

loss-plus-tax trap. The dilemma created when an investor seeks to avoid current long-term capital gains taxes on low basis investments instead of paying the taxes currently and implementing the consistent portfolio approach known as the Market Return Portfolio. This hesitation can lead to loss of value in the securities he/she is holding as well as an eventual tax on the remaining gain when the security is sold – thus creating a double loss situation.

market return. Nothing more, nothing less than the return readily available when investors efficiently harness the power of capital markets.

Market Return Benchmark. Designed to be a broader way to measure the success of the equity portion of a portfolio. The Market Return Benchmark is designed for individual investors. All other indexes were created as benchmarks for money managers. (See Appendix C for composition.)

Market Return Portfolio. A portfolio that is constructed with the objective of earning market return by using low-cost, no-load institutional asset class mutual funds.

misaligned interests. The financial interests of institutions and representatives who provide advice and investment products that are in conflict with the financial interests of the investor.

Modern Portfolio Theory (MPT). Research in finance over the last fifty-plus years that relates to the risk and return characteristics of various asset classes when they are combined to create investment portfolios. Academicians such as Harry Markowitz, William Sharpe, Merton Miller, Franco Modigliani, and Eugene Fama are some of the major contributors to this field of research.

proprietary products. Products designed and managed by institutions whose representatives then recommend them to investors. Proprietary products often have higher costs and steep penalties for selling, which keep investors tied to the products.

super-diversification. High degree of diversification that occurs when institutional asset class funds are used to construct a portfolio. IACFs provide broad and deep representation of the capital markets.

there for the taking. Idea that market return is accessible to all investors in a free capital market system.

Index I